D1710196

The Renaissance
EXPLORERS

With
**HISTORY
PROJECTS**
for Kids

Alicia Z. Klepeis

Nomad Press
A division of Nomad Communications
10 9 8 7 6 5 4 3 2 1

This book was manufactured by Friesens Book Division
Altona, MB, Canada
October 2018, Job #246260

ISBN Softcover: 978-1-61930-691-2
ISBN Hardcover: 978-1-61930-689-9

Educational Consultant, Marla Conn

Questions regarding the ordering of this book should be addressed to
Nomad Press
2456 Christian St.
White River Junction, VT 05001
www.nomadpress.net

Printed in Canada.

Titles in *The Renaissance for Kids* Series

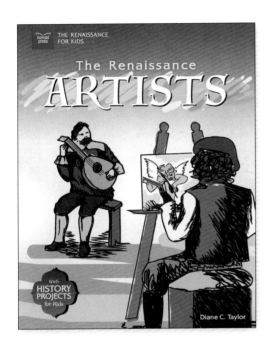

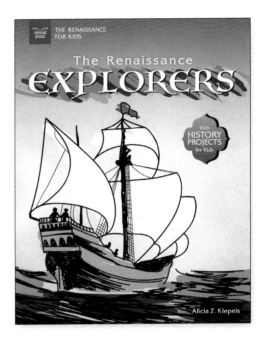

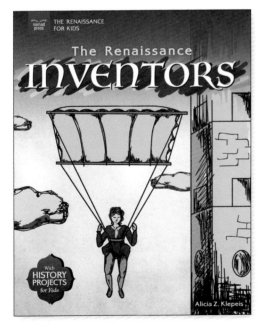

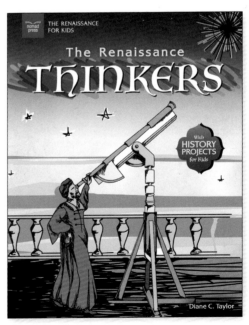

TABLE OF
Contents

A painting of a French seaport
By Claude Lorrain, 1639

EXPLORATION DURING THE
Renaissance

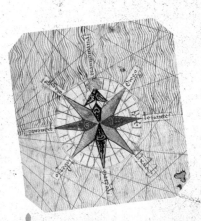

The first compass rose depicted on a map
By Abraham Cresques, 1375

Imagine boarding a ship and sailing off for lands unknown. Or disguising yourself to blend in with the local people as you explored new territories in search of exotic foods and goods. These were real situations for those brave enough to be explorers during the Renaissance.

FAST FACTS

WHAT:
THE RENAISSANCE, A HISTORICAL ERA MARKED BY DRAMATIC CHANGE

WHEN:
1300s–1600s

WHERE:
ITALY AND NORTHERN EUROPE

A map of Italy from 1584

The Renaissance took place in Europe between the fourteenth and seventeenth centuries. It started in Italy during the 1300s and spread north as far as England.

Renaissance Exploration
1300s–1600s

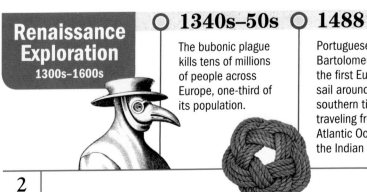

1340s–50s
The bubonic plague kills tens of millions of people across Europe, one-third of its population.

1488
Portuguese explorer Bartolomeu Dias is the first European to sail around Africa's southern tip, traveling from the Atlantic Ocean into the Indian Ocean.

1494
Spain and Portugal sign the Treaty of Tordesillas, dividing the New World into lands that could be claimed by one of these two European empires.

1497
Explorer John Cabot departs England and reaches the east coast of North America.

The Coliseum is an example of ancient Greek architecture.

What made the Renaissance so important that we still learn about it today? It was a time of new ideas, inventions, and scientific discovery. It was a period of people looking toward the past to connect with the possible future. People took chances and accomplished wonderful things.

During this period, there was a great renewal of interest in ancient Rome and Greece. Many of the leaders of the Renaissance, who were born in the different city-states of Italy, found inspiration in these ancient civilizations and wanted to know more by studying the art, architecture, and culture.

From Tough Times To New Discoveries

Many historians believe that the Renaissance was a response to the difficult years during the Middle Ages. This period, which came before the Renaissance, was tough for most people.

1500
Portuguese explorer Pedro Álvares Cabral travels across the Atlantic Ocean and reaches the coast of Brazil.

1508–12
Italian artist Michelangelo paints the ceiling of the Sistine Chapel.

1517
Martin Luther protests against the Catholic Church, starting the movement known as the Reformation.

1522
The first circumnavigation of the globe, begun by Ferdinand Magellan's fleet, is completed by Juan Sebastian Elcano.

1532
Spanish explorer Francisco Pizarro conquers the Inca Empire of Peru.

1570
The world's first atlas is published by Flemish cartographer Abraham Ortelius.

3

> "We have always been taught that navigation is the result of civilization, but modern archaeology has demonstrated very clearly that this is not so."
>
> **THOR HEYERDAHL (1914–2002), TWENTIETH-CENTURY NORWEGIAN ADVENTURER**

Imagine working in the fields all day, with very little time and freedom for fun. Imagine not having tasty, healthy food to eat or a comfortable house to live in. Imagine not being able to read! Books were rare during the Middle Ages and most were written in Latin, which was a language understood by only the most educated people in Europe.

The Catholic Church was the most powerful force during the Middle Ages. The pope, who was the head of the Church, was similar to a king. He could make rules and hand out punishments to anyone who didn't accept the teachings of the church.

The Middle Ages ended as people became more aware of life around the world. With the invention of the printing press, books became more common and more people learned to read. With trade and economic growth, many people escaped the life of a peasant, and more people traveled from their own small villages.

The Renaissance was a period of new discoveries. Brilliant ideas seemed to explode from Renaissance thinkers.

In both science and philosophy, people began to look beyond religion. They began to think of themselves as the center of the universe. This was a very new idea and called humanism.

WONDER WHY?

The word *renaissance* means "rebirth." It refers to the rebirth or renewal of interest in learning—about science, art, literature, architecture, and other fields of study. Are we experiencing another renaissance today? Why or why not?

CONNECT

You can learn about mapmaking from this video. How has mapmaking changed since the Renaissance? How might it improve in the future?

🔍 **TED age exploration**

Humanism was the new way of being interested in what other people were doing and thinking and creating. While people were still very religious during the Renaissance and the Church remained powerful, people began to think on their own about how the world worked.

Art & Architecture

Many amazing artists lived during the Renaissance. These included Leonardo da Vinci and Michelangelo. They created masterpieces that are celebrated even today.

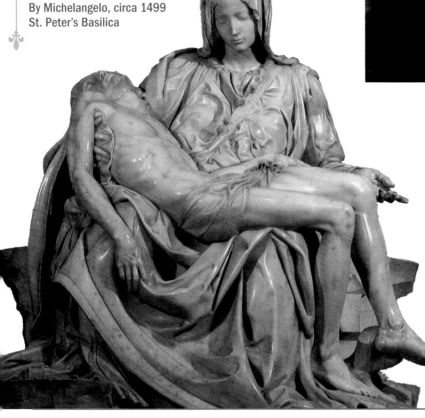

Pietà
By Michelangelo, circa 1499
St. Peter's Basilica

The *Mona Lisa*
By Leonardo da Vinci, 1503

Architects from this time, including Filippo Brunelleschi, used reason to solve the complicated challenges of building techniques. Today, tourists visiting the cities of Florence, Rome, and many other Italian cities will find lots of architecture and art from the Renaissance.

The Age of Discovery

During the Renaissance, some brilliant minds pursued knowledge through the study of math, art, and science. Other people expanded European knowledge by exploring the world.

Before the Renaissance, it was rare for people to venture far from home. Most people were peasants who farmed. Their day-to-day lives did not allow them much time for adventures. But during the Renaissance, explorers went on voyages of discovery. They traveled by water and over land to places previously not known to Europeans.

This fit in perfectly with the Renaissance emphasis on culture. Learning about the arts, customs, foods, and other achievements of people around the globe was an important part of exploration.

Many people use the term the "Age of Discovery" to refer to this period when many European expeditions traveled the globe. The Age of Discovery overlapped with the Renaissance.

The Dome of Brunelleschi on the Florence Cathedral

The dome was designed by Filippo Brunelleschi and completed in 1436. Drawn by Charles Herbert Moore, 1905

"Exploring is an innate part of being human. We're all explorers when we're born."

EDITH WIDDER (1951–), AMERICAN OCEANOGRAPHER AND MARINE BIOLOGIST

Why Did They Travel?

Why leave the comfort of home and family to strike out to new lands where danger might lurk? These men often were curious about the wider world beyond their homelands. They wanted to have adventures. Perhaps some hoped to gain fame.

TECHNOLOGY

Exploration goes hand in hand with the invention of new technology. Part of the reason explorers were able to travel farther from home had to do with advances in navigation and shipbuilding techniques.

When the Renaissance began, much of the world was a complete mystery to the people living in Europe. Maps made at the start of this period often look very little like those made at the end of the Renaissance. That's because of the tremendous efforts of fleets of explorers brave enough to sail into uncharted waters.

One of the most important reasons Europeans explored the world was to find a sea route to India and Asia. These regions were rich in spices of all kinds, as well as other exotic goods, including precious gems such as rubies and sapphires, fine silk used for fancy clothing, and new kinds of food.

Many of these luxury goods from India and the Far East were available before the Renaissance, but they were unbelievably expensive. Goods were brought by horse or camel caravan thousands of miles across Asia all the way to ports in the Middle East. Then, these items were taken to Europe by ship.

Along the way, Arabian and Turkish traders and merchants placed high taxes on these goods. By the time silk and spices arrived in European markets, they cost a fortune!

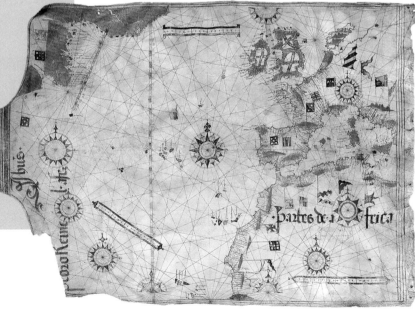

A nautical chart of the coastline of Europe

By Pedro Reinel, circa 1504

This camel is standing on the remains of the Silk Road, the path taken by ancient traders who traveled across Asia, Africa, and Europe.

credit: Jeanne Menjoulet (CC BY 2.0)

If European explorers could find sea routes to the Far East, they could avoid having to trade with the merchants and traders of Turkey and Arabia. Instead, Europeans could buy specialty items directly from Asian merchants and traders at better prices.

Efforts to reach the source of spices directly began during the Middle Ages. For example, the Vivaldi brothers of Genoa attempted to reach India by sailing around Africa in the late 1200s.

WONDER WHY?

Have you ever had an adventure traveling far from home? How did you handle being in a different place? Did you try different food and wear different clothes?

THE POWER OF SPICE

Have you ever eaten a cinnamon roll or put cinnamon sugar on your toast? Do your parents add pepper to a dish while cooking? For most of European history, these spices were not available to the average person outside of Asia, where they were grown. European explorers and traders hoped to get their hands on spices such as peppercorns, cloves, nutmeg, ginger, and cinnamon. These spices added flavor to food and some could be used as medicine.

European explorers and their patrons all hoped to gain wealth through these expeditions. While earning money through bringing luxury goods to Europe was one important motive in Renaissance explorations, there were other motives as well. Kings and queens who sponsored expeditions during the Age of Discovery also wanted to expand their empires.

GOLD IN THOSE HILLS!

If a European monarch gained control of new territory, they might gain access to valuable minerals, such as gold. Gold could be taken from its source back to Europe and made into coins to be used as currency. They could be saved for the future, building up the financial power of a European nation.

Religion and Exploration

Some European kings and queens were inspired to send expeditions out for religious reasons as well. Queen Isabella of Spain was one example.

She was a Christian ruler who wanted to spread Christianity to other parts of the world. On her expeditions, she sent missionaries to convert the indigenous peoples to Christianity. Why did she do this? She felt that it was part of her duty to God.

The Return of Christopher Columbus

Christopher Columbus reports to Queen Isabella and King Ferdinand, by Eugene Delacroix, 1839

Some European patrons of expeditions wanted to do more than just convert the local people to Christianity. They also wanted to defeat leaders who were not Christian.

Consider the tale of Portugal's Prince Henry the Navigator. Among his goals for the expeditions he sponsored was defeating Muslim rulers living in Africa. Unfortunately, goals such as this sometimes led to brutality between the European expedition members and the people they came into contact with.

Are You An Explorer?

Being a Renaissance explorer was exciting. There were new people to meet and new lands to discover.

It was also extremely dangerous. Storms could strike at any time. The navigation tools of the time were not nearly as sophisticated as the ones used on ships today. It was not uncommon for expeditions to lose ships that smashed against unseen rocks or icebergs.

Diseases often hit the explorers and their teams. Even if there was a doctor on board, the medicines and treatments of the time were not always effective.

WORDS OF WONDER

This book is packed with lots of new vocabulary! Try figuring out the meanings of unfamiliar words using the context and roots of the words. There is a glossary in the back to help you and Words of Wonder check-ins for every chapter.

In *The Renaissance Explorers*, you'll meet five famous explorers who traveled beyond the boundaries of the known world. These explorers were mostly men, but you'll also learn about several explorers who aren't as well known, including women and people of color. A member of an exploratory team in the Age of Discovery was likely to learn a lot and maybe get rich—can you imagine being a Renaissance explorer?

SAILOR FACTS

1 Sailors on Renaissance expeditions had only one set of clothing—which was very rarely washed!

2 The seamen working on Columbus's expeditions earned less than $10 per month in today's money.

3 Even though age 16 was really the minimum age for sailors, it was not uncommon for boys to begin working on ships as young as seven or eight years old.

Can You Guess the Scent?

Many of the world's most popular spices are grown in India. Can you guess what they are without peeking?

Caution: Only smell substances that you know won't hurt you. Always sniff gently so nothing goes up your nose.

➤ **Gather 5 to 10 different spices from India.** Some ideas include pepper (or whole peppercorns), cardamom, turmeric, cinnamon, mustard seed, ginger, cumin, clove, coriander, fennel, fenugreek, and saffron.

➤ **Label the bottoms of several paper cups with each spice.** Shake a tiny amount of each spice into its own labeled cup.

➤ **With a partner, take turns gently sniffing just above the top of the cup.** Be sure the person sniffing has their eyes closed. How many spices did you guess correctly?

➤ **Make a list of any foods or recipes you know that use spices from India.** With an adult's permission, prepare a meal using some of these spices. How does it taste? Why might people during the Renaissance be eager to buy these spices?

WRITE IT DOWN!

Many members of Renaissance expeditions kept journals. They recorded details about ocean and weather conditions. They took notes on the cultures of the people they met. They sketched the plants and animals they saw, sometimes even bringing back samples to Europe for further study. Do you keep a journal?

A map of the world by Venetian monk Fra Mauro. This image shows a reproduction made by W. Fraser in 1806. The map is oriented with south at the top.

CHAPTER 1

NICCOLÒ DE' Conti

Niccolò de' Conti was a merchant from Venice who traveled for 25 years through South and Southeast Asia, as well as through many places in the Middle East. The knowledge he gained while exploring provided scholars and mapmakers with new information about the people, animals, and landscapes of many lands previously unknown to Europeans.

Front cover of *Le Voyage Aux Indes* written by Niccolò de' Conti

FAST FACTS

BIRTH DATE:
CIRCA 1395

PLACE OF BIRTH:
CHIOGGIA, NEAR
VENICE, ITALY

AGE AT DEATH:
ABOUT 74, DIED 1469

FAMOUS
ACCOMPLISHMENT:
ONE OF THE FIRST
EUROPEANS TO REACH
INDONESIA AND
BURMA

A Teenager's Adventures

Almost nothing is known about Niccolò de' Conti's childhood and early years. We do know that he was born around 1395 in Chioggia, a coastal town near the southernmost end of the Venetian lagoon. Some sources say that his family had earned a lot of money from trading with people in Egypt.

While a young man, Conti lived in Damascus, a city in what is now the country of Syria, working as a merchant. Even as a young man, he realized something important—international trade offered incredible opportunities for adventure. Not to mention the chance to earn good money!

A detail from a 1459 map by Fra Mauro, based on observations by Niccolò de' Conti

Niccolò de' Conti 1395–1469	c. 1395	1414	1420 or 1421
	Conti is born in Chioggia, Italy.	Conti heads out from Damascus on his way to Baghdad.	Conti spends time in the Indian city of Vijayanagar.

Modern-day
Chioggia

EVERYTHING WE DON'T KNOW

For some people who lived long ago, we have plenty of information about when they did certain things. Conti, however, did not keep written records, and those who did write down his life story did not always get the dates right. Historians strive to fix previous errors made on Conti's timeline, but some of these dates may still be wrong. If someone were to make a timeline of your lifetime 100 years after you died, how would they know they were using the right dates? Why is accuracy important in the study of history?

Late 1420s–Early 1430s

He travels through Sumatra, Tenasserim, and the Irrawaddy basin.

1437

Conti arrives at Mount Sinai in Egypt and meets Pero Tafur.

1439

He tells the story of his journey to Poggio Bracciolini in Florence, Italy.

1469

Conti dies in Venice.

> "The tale of Conti's adventures was of absorbing interest to geographers, but it was hardly likely to excite investors. The way he had gone was too dangerous for regular profitable trade, and he had no suggestions about alternative routes."
>
> HISTORIAN J.H. PARRY (1914–1982)

While in Damascus, Conti learned the Arabic language. This was essential to his success as a traveler and a merchant. Why? Being able to speak Arabic meant that he could communicate with local people and blend in more as well. In 1414, while he was still a teenager, Conti headed toward the city of Baghdad, in the country now known as Iraq.

He made this journey as part of an Arab caravan. Traveling as part of a group was much safer for Conti. Plus, it was far less lonely! Back then, Europeans rarely traveled in this region, and those who did usually joined a group of Persians or Arabs.

Conti was part of a caravan of about 600 other merchants. It would have been a mistake for robbers to attack such a large group.

Conti's route across the Indian Ocean

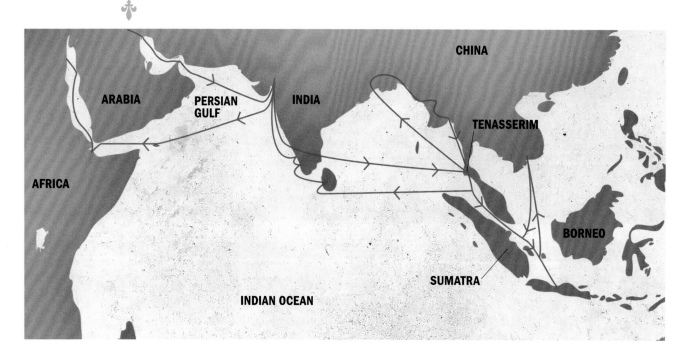

With this huge caravan, Conti traveled through the deserts of a region called Arabia Petraea. This area once belonged to the Roman Empire. Today, it includes parts of Syria, Jordan, Saudi Arabia, and the Negev region.

Like all explorers, Conti had his share of adventures and misadventures. One took place while in Arabia Petraea. One night, around midnight, he and his fellow merchants were resting in the desert. Suddenly, they heard a noise. They leapt to their feet, worried that they were being robbed.

A huge stream of people on horseback passed right by their tents, making hardly any sound. The strangers did not bother Conti's caravan. Other merchants who'd had something similar happen to them described such passersby as "demons," though in truth they weren't behaving badly. It was simply a bizarre encounter in the Arabian desert.

FUN FESTIVALS

Part of an explorer's job is learning about other cultures. While in India, Conti was able to observe several festivals. One festival took place in the temples and on the roofs of people's homes. This event involved people lighting "an innumerable number" of oil lamps, which burned both day and night. Another festival Conti mentioned lasted for nine days. Part of the celebrations involved a rather unusual event—each day, a holy man would sit atop a tall beam, like a ship mast. While the men were on their perches, other folks would throw lemons, oranges, and other highly scented fruits at these patient religious men. The holy men would also pray for God's favor during this festival time. What are some rituals people perform today around the world? Do any of them seem strange to you?

"There be in that Countrey daungerous Serpents, of six cubites in length, and as thicke as a man, having no feete. The people of that Countrey, have great delight in eating of those Serpents rosted."

NICCOLÒ DE' CONTI

Partnering with the Persians

After trekking through Arabia Petraea, Conti traveled down the Tigris River and reached the Persian port city of Hormuz. This area lies close to the southern end of the Persian Gulf, and is now part of Iran. Hormuz was bustling with trade.

Conti continued his adventures in Persia, venturing to the coastal trading center of Calacatia, where he spent a chunk of time. He learned the local language, Persian, during his time in Hormuz. While in Calacatia, Conti started to dress like the local people of the area.

The Bibi Maryam mausoleum near the ancient city of Qalhat

credit:
Alfred Weidinger
(CC BY 2.0)

THE CITY OF QALHAT

Among the sites that Niccolò de' Conti visited while in the area of the Persian Gulf is the city of Qalhat. This harbor city is located on the Gulf of Oman. It was an important port for many centuries and welcomed ships traveling through the Arabian Sea from Yemen, India, and Dhofar. Qalhat was a rich city, with an impressive bazaar and lots of activity. Dates, salt, and pearls were just some of the products exported from this area. The mosque in Qalhat was famous and quite large. Wealthy merchants lived in fancy homes here. Visitors to the city today can see the remains of an ancient mausoleum.

He continued to wear this style of clothing throughout the rest of his travels. Dressing like the local people allowed explorers to blend in better while traveling.

> "Thys River Gangey is of such breadth, that Sayling in the middest, you shall see no lande on neyther side, and hee affynneth that it is in some places fifteene myles in breadth."
>
> **NICCOLÒ DE' CONTI**

Conti decided to join a group of Persian merchants for the next stretch of his explorations. Conti and his new partners pledged to be loyal and faithful companions to each other.

It was important to trust the people one was traveling with, especially when journeying into foreign lands, where conflict with others was a very real possibility. Have you ever traveled with people you don't really know or trust? What was it like?

Along with his Persian travel companions, Niccolò de' Conti boarded a ship bound for India. Who knew what adventures lay ahead?

India: A Land of Many Discoveries

After sailing east with his Persian companions for about a month, Niccolò de' Conti finally landed on the subcontinent of India. He first arrived in the city of Cambay, located in northwestern India.

While traveling through India, Conti witnessed many customs and traditions that were different from those he was familiar with as a Venetian man. For example, he learned that it was the custom for an Indian wife to burn herself on the funeral pyre of her husband! This was not how people mourned back in Italy.

WONDER WHY?

Throughout history, people have been both amazed and horrified at some of the customs they've encountered while traveling. Have you ever had this experience? Did it make you question any of your own traditions?

After his time in Cambay, Conti traveled by ship down the Indian coast for 20 days. He arrived at two different Indian cities—Pacamuria (thought to be modern-day Barkur) and Helly (perhaps Mount d'Ely or Cabo d'Ely). In the area around these cities, he learned about the ginger plant.

Conti probably saw the way that ginger was dried in the sun as part of its preparation. Describing plants and animals unfamiliar to most Europeans was one way that Renaissance explorers such as Niccolò de' Conti were able to bring the world to others.

Who might be interested in learning about ginger? Many people benefitted from the knowledge shared by explorers—doctors interested in medicines, cooks looking for new flavors, anyone with a sense of curiosity.

From Pacamuria and Helly, Conti traveled about 300 miles inland into India. He arrived at a city he called Bizenegalia, now known as Vijayanagar. The year was 1420 or 1421.

Virupaksha, a seventh-century Hindu temple in Vijayanagar

credit: Jean-Pierre Dalbéra (CC BY 2.0)

THE WIVES AND FAMILIES OF EXPLORERS

Renaissance explorers often left Europe with no idea how long they'd be gone. Some of these explorers were married. Yet it was very unusual for the wives to travel with their adventurous husbands. During the Renaissance, most women stayed at home and took care of their households and their children. Rarely did women travel outside their own country. However, there were some exceptions to this tradition. John Cabot (dates unknown) was a Renaissance explorer from Italy. His wife was from Venice. She traveled with Cabot to London, England, as did their children. Niccolò de' Conti's wife, who he met in India, and family also accompanied him on some of his travels, including to Cairo, Egypt. In fact, his four children were born during the course of his many exploratory journeys. How might Conti's experience as an explorer have been different as a result of having his family with him?

Conti described the city as being located near very steep mountains, but some modern writers describe it as being made up of rocky hills.

Of course, not every description provided by an explorer is always 100-percent accurate. Niccolò de' Conti did not write his own book about his explorations. Instead, other people who listened to his adventurous tales wrote down his descriptions and stories. In this way, descriptions often changed, sometimes quite a lot.

Conti was fascinated by the power of the king living in Bizenegalia. He was said to be more powerful than any other in the whole of India. It was also said that this king had thousands of wives.

Certainly this was very different from the lives of kings in Europe. Conti was also impressed by this city's walls and military power.

Pearls, Paper, and a Wife

Niccolò de' Conti continued his explorations of India. Among the many cities he visited was Malepur. This city was famous for its large, beautiful church, where the body of St. Thomas was buried.

Malepur and the nearby city of Cahlia, which Conti visited, were both in Malabar province. As explorers often did, Conti reported on many of the natural phenomena he came across in the area. One example was pearls, which were found in the city of Cahlia.

21

EXCITING NEW FRUITS

Trying new foods was an essential part of survival for Renaissance explorers. After all, the food that these men brought with them was not enough to feed them for their entire journeys. In Malabar, Conti tried the fruit of the jack tree. He described it as sweet in taste, similar in appearance to the pineapple, and so big that it could be difficult for one man to lift. He also tasted mango, which he compared in sweetness to honey. Of course, it was helpful for explorers to have local people show them what was edible. Otherwise, they might not have made it back home again!

WONDER WHY?

Would you rather explore new lands as part of an organized expedition or with your family? Why?

Conti also described a plant that had leaves that were six cubits, or roughly 9 feet long. Despite their huge size, the leaves were thin enough to hold in your hand if folded. They could be used as protection during a rainstorm. People also wrote on them, instead of paper. This plant was some kind of palm.

While many Renaissance explorers were older when they traveled the world, Niccolò de' Conti was still a young man when he arrived in India. Many sources mention that he married an Indian woman, though there are few details about her. We do know the couple had children together and traveled together.

> "There is in that Countrey a certayne kinde of fruit, like unto the Orenge, whiche they doe call Cyeno, full of juice and sweetenesse."
>
> **NICCOLÒ DE' CONTI**

Sumatra . . . and People Eaters!

Despite gaining much knowledge (and a wife!) in India, Niccolò de' Conti did not stay there. He continued to head east rather than go home to Italy. He traveled to the island of Sumatra, which today is part of the country of Indonesia. Conti was among the earliest European explorers to set foot on this huge island. According to several historical accounts, he stayed on Sumatra for an entire year.

As was his habit wherever he journeyed, Conti explored the natural resources of Sumatra. He mentioned gold being abundant on the island. He also saw different types of pepper. The durian fruit, highly prized in this region, was yet another new food to try.

Durian fruit

The smell of durians is so strong that, today, some countries ban the fruit from public transportation and even hotel lobbies!

The camphor tree was another fascinating example of plant life unfamiliar to Europeans. The resin of this tree was highly sought after by early Arab traders. It was used for both perfumes and incense. In fact, at some points in history, certain varieties of camphor were worth as much as gold.

CONNECT

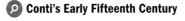

You can read some of Conti's observations on his travels at this website. What kinds of things does he describe? Would a modern-day traveler notice the same things?

🔍 **Conti's Early Fifteenth Century**

Besides reporting on natural discoveries, Niccolò de' Conti also had much to say about the people of Sumatra and their customs. He commented about some of the different practices of the people, including cannibalism.

Conti mentions that in one part of the island, people were constantly battling one another and saving the heads of fallen enemies. Why? These heads were considered valuable and were traded for other items.

From Burma to Borneo

Setting sail from Sumatra, Conti spent more than two weeks at sea. Conditions were stormy and it was rough going. But Conti arrived at Tenasserim, which was part of what was known for centuries as Burma and is today known as Myanmar. He is said to be the first European to visit Tenasserim. Conti described it as having an abundance of elephants. While in Tenasserim, he traveled by boat down the Irrawaddy River. He also visited Ava, the capital city of the kingdom.

Myanmar today

Until Conti's time, no European explorer had ever left any records of visiting either the interior of Burma or its coastline. Conti also stopped at the wealthy port city of Pegu in southern Burma. This city was the capital of the Mon kingdom for centuries, as well as a center for Buddhist culture.

Niccolò de' Conti explored many parts of the Indonesian archipelago, including the islands of Java and Borneo. A number of sources say that he spent about nine months on Borneo, the third-largest island in the world.

Because this island was farther away from Indian trade routes and from the rest of the Malay Peninsula, it was not a frequent destination of traders.

With its wet, hot climate, Borneo has some of the most diverse plant life on Earth. Conti was able to observe many plants unknown to Europeans. He described a number of crops grown here, including nutmeg and durian.

Proboscis monkeys in Borneo

The information Conti gathered greatly helped to improve the Asian portion of a famous map known as the "Genoese map," produced sometime between 1447 and 1457. Conti also used his knowledge of the Indonesian islands to help a monk named Fra Mauro create a world map in 1459.

Just how far east did Niccolò de' Conti go? The Indonesian islands of Java and Borneo were the end of the line for this brave explorer.

It was while on Borneo that Conti heard from other traders about the Moluccas, also known as the Spice Islands. But Conti had traveled far and long and it was time to return to Italy. He'd even traveled far enough east to be the first European traveler to report seeing a bird of paradise, which live only on the island of New Guinea and adjacent islands.

The author of the Genoese map is unknown

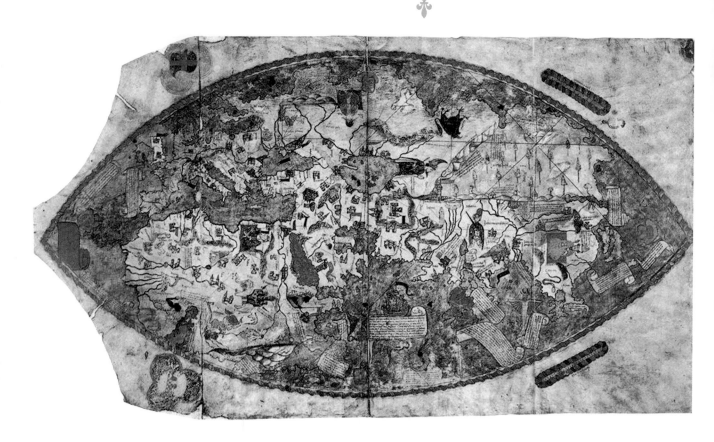

The Journey Home

On his way back to Italy, Niccolò de' Conti had many more adventures on land and by sea. Some of his stops were places he hadn't seen yet, such as Ciampa, which is perhaps in what is now Thailand. Others were locations he'd already visited, including Cambay in India.

From Cambay, Conti headed for the southern coast of the Arabian Peninsula and the city of Aden. He stopped in Jidda, the port that served Mecca. In 1437, Conti made an especially important connection with a person he met near Mount Sinai. He was a Spanish nobleman named Pero Tafur (1410–1487).

WONDER WHY?

Do you think if more European explorers were familiar with the local languages in the places they visited, their experiences would have been different? If so, how?

"Conti's descriptions of spices in the East Indies greatly spurred the pace of European exploration."

WRITER JUDSON KNIGHT (1964–)

Tafur joined Conti's caravan, staying with Conti and his family on the 15-day trip to Cairo. They traveled together for several more weeks while they visited the many sights of that city. Conti and his wife now had four children, who had all been born on the journey!

During this time, Conti told Tafur of his many travel adventures. Tafur recorded these stories and turned them into a book called *Travels and Adventures, 1435-1439*. Tafur's book tended to focus on the unusual sights, people, and animals that Conti had encountered. The stories in this book tend to be quite random, rather than an organized description of new lands.

Tragedy struck Niccolò de' Conti while in Egypt. His wife and two of his children died during an epidemic. They were killed by a disease known as the plague.

Details are sketchy about another stressful situation Conti experienced in Egypt. The explorer is said to have been in Cairo when his life was threatened because he was a Christian. During this episode, Conti renounced his faith as a way to "save his skin," according to some sources. This event had important consequences when Conti finally arrived back in Venice around 1439.

Abandoning the Christian faith was considered sinful. But Conti was given the chance to make amends for his wrongdoing. As penance, he had to tell about all his adventures to the secretary of Pope Eugenius IV (1383–1447), a man named Gian Francesco Poggio Bracciolini (1380–1459).

In 1439, Bracciolini wrote down this narrative in Latin in the Italian city of Florence. Bracciolini provides a valuable account of what it was like in southern Asia during the fifteenth century. The book, *On the Vicissitudes of Fortune*, became a tremendous source for future explorers, traders, and scientists.

In Conti's later years, he took part in a number of trade missions across Italy with the task of buying oil and cereals. He died in 1469.

What Makes Him Different?

Niccolò de' Conti is different from other Renaissance explorers in several ways. For one thing, he was not sponsored by a king or queen. Instead, he was a self-funded explorer looking for a new trade route to Asia, as well as for opportunities to make money through trade with people in far-flung locations.

WHO WAS ZHENG HE?

You may have heard of Christopher Columbus or Ferdinand Magellan? How about an explorer named Zheng He (1371–1433)? Born in China, Zheng He was a brave and adventurous explorer who many people have never heard of! He went on seven different voyages as the commander of what was known as the Treasure Fleet. Built at the direction of Emperor Zhu Di (1360–1424), this fleet of ships included warships, trading ships, and support vessels. Zheng He's first voyage with the Treasure Fleet started in 1405. He died in 1433 while on his seventh voyage. While leading the fleet, he and his men explored and traded across both Africa and Asia. Zheng He's expedition brought many special goods back to China, from gemstones to spices to beautiful carpets. He is remembered for establishing Chinese trading relationships with Africa, Arabia, India, and Southeast Asia.

The plague was feared around the world, as epidemics frequently broke out and killed many people.

A lithograph by G. Gallina after A. Manzoni

credit: Wellcome Library no. 6412i (CC BY 4.0)

Another difference is the length of Conti's travels. Unlike most other Renaissance explorers, Conti traveled for about 25 years straight without coming home at all during that time! His itinerary was unbelievably extensive, and included destinations unknown to most Europeans of the time.

In addition, Conti's knowledge of Arabic and Persian was unusual. His language abilities allowed him to live more easily in trading communities operated by Muslims around the Indian Ocean.

Language skills and his adoption of a non-European style of dress probably enhanced his ability to travel on ships that were owned by Muslim merchants.

Unlike earlier explorers such as Marco Polo (1254–1324), Conti didn't write his own memoir of his explorations. Instead, the writings based on his travels were created by others who hadn't been part of his adventures, such as Tafur and Bracciolini.

```
IOS          XII.
FLORENT.  IOAN  FRANCISC
POGGIVS
Felle armata tibi manus est, multoq; cachinno
Tinxisti et nudo scripta proterva sale.
```

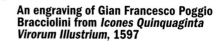

An engraving of Gian Francesco Poggio Bracciolini from *Icones Quinquaginta Virorum Illustrium*, 1597

By Jean Jacques Boissard (1528–1602)

Lasting Legacy

Niccolò de' Conti was one of the first Europeans to make it to Indonesia. He also contributed much information about the people, spices, animals , and geography of the lands he traveled through when he described his travels to Poggio Bracciolini. Most Europeans knew practically nothing of the people and wildlife of many of the regions Conti visited, especially Burma and what is now Indonesia.

The information from Conti's travels influenced the earliest two maps of the Malaysia and Borneo region created in Europe during the 1450s. The tales of far-off lands that he brought back to Italy made others want to see the plants, birds, and people that he described.

WORDS OF WONDER

What vocabulary words did you discover? Can you figure out the meanings of these words by using the context and roots? Look in the glossary for help!

cannibalism · caravan · lagoon
merchant · culture · subcontinent

What You Need

a small paper clip, a magnet, an ice-cube-sized piece of Styrofoam or cork, a bowl, water

Make a Compass

The compass has been an essential tool to explorers for many centuries. It helped to determine which direction they were heading! Compasses are not dependent on the weather. Some sources say that the world's first practical compass was made in Venice in the late thirteenth century.

> **Bend the paper clip until it looks like a straight line.**

> **Rub the magnet against the paper clip at least 50 times.** Be sure to rub the magnet in the same direction each time.

> **Very carefully push the paper clip all the way through the piece of Styrofoam or cork.**

> **Fill your bowl at least halfway up the sides with water.**

> **Gently place the paper clip and Styrofoam onto the water's surface.** Give it a minute to align itself with the earth's magnetic fields. It will soon point north. What happens when you blow on the paper clip?

> **Face north.** Can you figure out each of the directions—west, east, and south?

Try This!

> **Draw a map of your neighborhood, using the directions you know from your compass.** Then, write directions for someone from your house to the store or library or another point of reference. Use north, south, east, and west instead of left and right. Is it difficult? Can someone else follow your directions?

BARTOLOMEU DIAS 1450-1500

CHAPTER 2

BARTOLOMEU
Dias

Details from a 1991 Portuguese bank note with Bartolomeu Dias's image (left and above)

Bartolomeu Dias was a Portuguese explorer. He was the first European explorer to sail around the southern tip of the African continent, traveling from the Atlantic Ocean to the Indian Ocean. His explorations proved that it was possible to travel by sea from Europe to Asia. Dias's adventures opened new opportunities for those seeking to trade with people in India.

FAST FACTS

BIRTH DATE:
1450

PLACE OF BIRTH:
ALGARVE, PORTUGAL

AGE AT DEATH: 50,
DIED 1500

FAMOUS ACCOMPLISHMENT:
THE FIRST PERSON FROM EUROPE TO SAIL AROUND THE SOUTHERN TIP OF AFRICA

Early Life

Not much is known about Bartolomeu Dias's childhood. In 1450, he was born near Portugal's capital city, Lisbon. Because he was raised in a noble family, he probably received a good quality education.

WONDER WHY?

Why were richer families better educated? Do you think this still holds true today? Why or why not? How does your family's level of wealth and class influence your own life? Do you think this is fair?

"Dias made a greater contribution to the discovery of the sea route to India than any other individual navigator."

HISTORIAN ERIC AXELSON (1913–1998)

What kinds of jobs did Dias have in his early life? Opinions differ about this. Some sources say he worked in the royal warehouses for the king of Portugal. Others say he was a squire of the royal household. Squires were young noblemen, typically between 14 and 21 years old. They served as attendants to knights before becoming knights themselves. Squires helped knights in combat or when traveling. They packed bags, cleaned armor, and took care of horses.

When he was old enough, Dias became a knight in the Portuguese royal court. It was during his time as a knight that Dias was given the chance to lead a new expedition.

Bartolomeu Dias
1450–1500

1450
Dias is born in Algarve, Portugal.

1487
In August, Dias leaves Lisbon with three ships and the goal to reach India.

1488
He returns to Portugal after more than 16 months at sea. He rounds the tip of South Africa but does not reach India.

Portugal's Maritime History

During Dias's life, Portugal was a strong seafaring nation. Portuguese explorers were actively exploring Africa with the goal of finding a trade route around Africa that would take Portuguese sailors and merchants from Europe to Asia. Before Dias's time, many attempts were made to find such a route. But none were successful.

Whenever people today talk about Portugal's maritime history, the first name that usually comes to mind is Prince Henry the Navigator (1394–1460). Many experts consider him to be largely responsible for Portugal's impressive age of exploration—even though he didn't do much sailing himself!

Between about 1419 and 1460, Prince Henry sent several sailing expeditions down Africa's west coast. Prince Henry died when Bartolomeu Dias was just a boy. But Henry's successor, King John II (1455–1495), had similar goals for exploration.

WHO WAS PRESTER JOHN?

Among the many goals of Bartolomeu Dias's expedition was making contact with a legendary Christian figure named Prester John, famous through several medieval accounts. He was said to be a Christian ruler with a kingdom in the East beyond Persia and Armenia, perhaps in Ethiopia. Many Europeans considered Prester John both a protector of Christians and an ally against Muslims. Several European expeditions sought to connect with this leader. Perhaps he could help Portuguese explorers convert Muslims in Africa to Christianity, aiding the Portuguese in their goal to establish control over Africa and its natural resources.

1494
King Manuel I appoints Dias to supervise construction of ships for Vasco da Gama's expedition to India.

1497
Dias travels on an expedition with Vasco da Gama, but only as far as the Cape Verde Islands.

March 1500
Dias joins the fleet of explorer Pedro Álvares Cabral, en route to India.

May 1500
Dias dies when his ship is lost at sea off the coast of South Africa.

No detailed accounts exist to tell us when and where Dias gained his experience as a sailor and navigator. In 1481, he went on a trip with Diogo de Azambuja (1432–1518), a nobleman. They voyaged down to what was called Africa's Gold Coast, now located in the country of Ghana.

In October 1486, King John II appointed Dias as the leader of an expedition. Its mission? To finally find a trade route by sea to India.

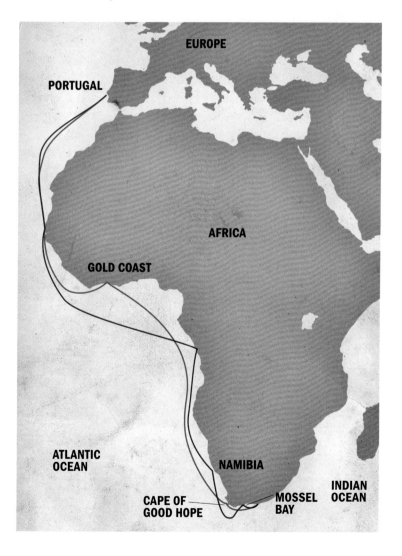

Preparations

Dias spent more than 10 months preparing for the trip, and left Lisbon in 1487. He had a supply ship and two armed caravels named the *São Cristóvão* and the *São Pantaleão* with him.

Caravels were small but fast ships popularly used between the fifteenth and seventeenth centuries. Unlike the typical ships of the time with big, round bottoms, the caravels featured shallower keels and slimmer hulls.

Caravels were built for speed and maneuverability. They could get in and out of inlets and shallow harbors easily. For this reason they were perfect for coastal exploration.

Dias's path of exploration
The blue line is the journey out and the red line is the journey homeward.

Space was tight on these ships, so supplies had to be chosen carefully. Dias had learned from explorer Diogo Cão (1450–1486) that there were few places to get provisions when traveling along southwest Africa's dry coast. Dias brought weapons and food. His ships also included items you'd never expect!

Among the unusual supplies were padrãos. These were stone crosses carved with the king of Portugal's name and the royal coat of arms.

BARTHOLOMEW DIAZ ON HIS VOYAGE TO THE CAPE.

An 1887 illustration of Bartolomeu Dias and his two caravels, from the book, *The Sea: Its Stirring Story of Adventure, Peril & Heroism, Volume 2*

WONDER WHY?

How do you think indigenous people felt when explorers from other countries claimed their land, even when these local people already lived there? How did they feel when explorers started settlements, colonizing these claimed lands. When are some other times colonization has happened in history? Does it ever happen today?

Explorers such as Dias placed the padrãos along the coastlines they explored to claim the land for Portugal. The padrãos also served as markers to show where previous expeditions had been.

Dias's Big Voyage

In August 1487, Dias and his crew set sail from Lisbon. Dias himself commanded the *São Cristóvão*. He planned to follow the route taken by fellow Portuguese explorer Cão. Cão had made it down the west coast of Africa as far south as what is now known as Cape Cross in Namibia.

At first, Dias headed for the mouth of the mighty Congo River. Along the way, the expedition stopped to pick up provisions at a Portuguese fort in the fishing port of Elmina, located on the Gold Coast.

Things went quite smoothly for Dias's expedition, which continued to travel southward along the African coast. On December 8, 1487, Dias arrived at Walvis Bay, Namibia. And on December 26, he reached Elizabeth Bay in southern Namibia. In the tradition of explorers before him, Dias ordered that a padrão be erected about 300 miles south of Walvis Bay. Today, this spot is known as Dias Point.

Sometime in early January 1488, times got tough. Fierce storms hit. Dias ordered his ships to go farther out to sea in the hope that they could avoid being shipwrecked. They spent 13 days caught in the storm.

A replica of the original Dias cross at Dias Point on the Lüderitz Peninsula, Namibia
credit: Damien du Toit (CC BY 2.0)

WHO WERE THE AFRICANS TRAVELING WITH DIAS'S EXPEDITION?

Bartolomeu Dias's expedition included six people from Africa. The two men and four women were from what is today Guinea and Angola. They were hostages who'd been brought to Portugal by other explorers, including Diogo Cão. The plan was for Dias's ships to drop them off at various ports on Africa's west coast. They could serve as interpreters between the Portuguese explorers and the native peoples of Africa. These African members of Dias's company would bring samples of silver, gold, and spices to the people they visited and ask where other samples of these products could be found. They also were supposed to share goodwill messages from Portugal with the local people. They'd been instructed to praise Portugal's king and tell the local kings and chiefs that the Portuguese king hoped to establish relations with a legendary figure known as Prester John. How do you think the African people aboard Dias's fleet felt while on board the ships and when they were dropped off at various destinations in Africa? Do you think these people benefitted from being part of the expedition? Why or why not?

> "We were hit by very strong headwinds that drove us out to sea. With no land in sight, we were forced to head south for almost two weeks. We then headed eastward in hopes of finding the shore. Only after this entire ordeal did I realize that we must already have sailed past the most southern tip of Africa."
>
> **BARTOLOMEU DIAS**

Eventually, the weather cleared up. Dias now sailed east—he wanted to see land again. He had no luck sailing east so he turned north instead. He found the coast, but something had changed dramatically. Instead of the land going from north to south, the coastline now followed a path from west to east!

How was this possible? In the chaos of trying to get through the storms and find his way, Bartolomeu Dias had sailed around the southern tip of Africa—without even knowing it!

On February 3, 1488, he landed on the coast of what is now South Africa in a place called Mossel Bay.

Dias continued to sail. On March 12, he arrived at a place now called Algoa Bay. Dias really wanted to forge ahead and get to India. All his officers, however, wanted to head home to Portugal. They agreed to travel for a few more days, and reached what's now known as the Great Fish River, or Rio do Infante. Dias left another stone-cross marker near this river.

Without the support of his crew, Bartolomeu Dias had no choice but to return to Europe. It was on the return journey, in May 1488, that Dias found what is today known as the Cape of Good Hope, close to Africa's southern tip. He had not seen it on the way down because of the storms!

CONNECT

Watch a reenactment of Dias's voyage and learn more about the caravel ships he built and sailed.

 Dias's caravel Hatchuel

Cape of
Good Hope

Does it seem strange that such a stormy and treacherous area is named the Cape of Good Hope? After all, this stretch of water is famous for wrecking ships.

At first, Dias named it the Cape of Storms because of the many violent storms in the area. But King John II decided to give it a less frightening name. He hoped more people would travel in that direction in the future. It turned out to be another nine years before the next Portuguese sailors made it around the cape again.

WONDER WHY?

Would you want to travel to a place called the Cape of Storms? Would you feel better about your trip knowing you were going to a place called the Cape of Good Hope? Why might the name be an important part of choosing a place to travel to?

When did the expedition finally get home? December 1488. Dias and his crew had been gone for more than 16 months.

More Adventures for Dias

There is some debate over the reception Dias received when he got back to Portugal. Some say the king was unhappy that the expedition never made it to India and that it never met up with Prester John. Others say that King John II immediately made plans for another voyage around the Cape of Good Hope, but that he died before this expedition came to be.

Bartolomeu Dias did not receive much reward for all his hard work leading the expedition. After the journey, Dias lived for a while in West Africa in an area now known as Guinea. It was the location of a gold-trading site established by the Portuguese.

In 1494, Dias was given a new assignment by King John II's successor, King Manuel I (1469–1521). His new job was to be a shipbuilding consultant for another Portuguese expedition, commanded by Vasco da Gama (c. 1460–1524).

VERONICA GAMBARA

During the Renaissance, women did not lead expeditions around the globe like Dias did. But that doesn't mean women of the Renaissance never traveled or had adventures. Born in Italy in 1485, Veronica Gambara became a well-known poet in her home country. She was the wife of the lord of Corregio. After he died in 1518, she became ruler of the land. She became involved in politics, corresponding on behalf of peace with leaders such as Spanish emperor Charles V. She was particularly involved in working on the military defense of Corregio. In the 1520s and 1530s, Gambara's travels took her to many of Italy's great cities, including Parma, Venice, Ferrara, and Bologna. In her later years, she traveled even more. Gambara has been described as "one of the first poet-rulers of the Early Modern Italian tradition."

You might think this post was a real disappointment after heading his own expedition. Nevertheless, Dias successfully oversaw the construction of two new ships, the *São Raphael* and *São Gabriel*.

These ships were stronger and bigger than those used for his own expedition. Their sails were square rather than triangular, which made the ships faster in the open ocean.

> "This expedition around the cape provided me with priceless information for future journeys of exploration, and the promise of creating direct trading routes from Portugal to India."
>
> **BARTOLOMEU DIAS**

When Vasco da Gama headed out for his famous expedition to India in 1497, Bartolomeu Dias accompanied him. However, Dias traveled with the expedition only as far as the Cape Verde Islands. There, he left da Gama's fleet and headed to Elmina, in Ghana.

Bartolomeu Dias's days as a navigator were not over, however. He also sailed on an expedition with another famous explorer, Pedro Álvares Cabral (1467–1520). This expedition was headed to India, though it took a different route than Dias had taken years before.

Storms forced Cabral's fleet off course. This was always a potential danger for sailors in these early voyages of discovery. Unlike today's modern vessels, these fifteenth-century ships did not have instruments such as GPS to help them figure out their location!

On April 22, 1500, Cabral's expedition ended up landing on the southeastern coast of what is now Brazil. Cabral's fleet had been blown more than 1,000 miles off its intended course!

Sadly, just a month later, Dias died. His ship was one of four lost at sea near the Cape of Good Hope. He was 50 years old.

WONDER WHY?

How might Dias's life and legacy been different if his team members had decided to keep traveling to India rather than turning back and going home after the terrible storms?

What Makes Him Different?

Bartolomeu Dias was different from some of the other Renaissance explorers in various ways. For one thing, while some sources say that he came from a seafaring family, Dias did not spend his early life at sea.

A statue of Dias in Trafalgar Square, London, England

Even though explorers had to be very familiar with how their sailing vessels worked, they didn't necessarily have shipbuilding skills. But Bartolomeu Dias supervised the construction of ships for Vasco da Gama's expedition. This was not a job that most former expedition leaders or commanders typically did.

From navigation to the management of crews and supplies to shipbuilding, Dias was a very well-rounded explorer.

Lasting Legacy

Bartolomeu Dias was an essential part of Portugal's age of exploration. He showed that there was a southern end to Africa and that the Atlantic and Indian Oceans were linked.

Dias's expedition made it clear that you could get to India by traveling around the southern tip of Africa. Armed with this new knowledge, more European merchants and explorers created their own maritime trade routes to India and Asia.

WORDS OF WONDER

What vocabulary words did you discover? Can you figure out the meanings of these words by using the context and roots? Look in the glossary for help!

caravel · maritime · maneuverability
padrãos · provisions · squire

Build a Caravel

When Bartolomeu Dias made his famous expedition, caravels were some of the fastest ships around. In this activity, you will design and make a caravel.

> **At the library or, with an adult's permission, on the internet, do some research on fifteenth-century caravels.** What did they look like? What shape were they? What did their sails look like? Where in the boat could people go?

> **Sketch some ideas on what you want your own caravel to look like.** Do you want to follow the same designs as Bartolomeu Dias? How can you design your ship so that it floats well and can turn easily?

> **Once you have a sketch you like, brainstorm materials.** What will you use for the ship's body? What will you use for sails? What kinds of materials do you have now that are similar to what Dias had back in the Renaissance? Some ideas for supplies are shoeboxes, modeling clay, duct tape, craft foam, bamboo skewers, and cork.

> **Start building with the supplies you gathered!** It might take several tries to get a model that you're happy with.

> **Once you have a design you like, test it out in the bathtub.** Does it float? Does it turn easily? Does it wobble back and forth a lot? What design changes can you make to fix any problems?

Try This!

> **Do some research on the kinds of ships being built today.** How are they different from a caravel? How are they similar?

Write a Journal

Being a member of Bartolomeu Dias's expedition was exciting. Sometimes, it was stressful, such as when caught in a storm or running low on food supplies. Other times, it was terrific, as when discovering new travel routes or seeing unfamiliar plants and animals.

> **Imagine that you are a shipmate on Dias's 1487–1488 trip from Portugal to South Africa and back.** Write a journal entry about some of your experiences.

> **Start by researching Dias's expedition.** Read some historical accounts of the voyage. You can use books or, with an adult's permission, the internet.

> **Choose one location from Dias's itinerary to write about.** It could be a place out at sea or on land. For example, the expedition traveled to the Portuguese fortress São Jorge de Mina. It also visited the Golfo da Conceição (called Walvis Bay today).

> **As if you are a member of Dias's team, write a journal entry about what is happening at the place you chose.** You could be one of the fellow fleet commanders, a young sailor, or even a cook. Describe the events with as much detail as you can. Think of including sensory details—what you see, smell, taste, or hear.

Try This!

> **Draw a picture of the scene you are describing.** Do you find it easier to convey your ideas with words or with art? Do you think early explorers drew pictures in their journals? Do some research and see if you can find any Renaissance doodles!

Vasco da Gama, circa 1460–1524
By Antonio Manuel da Fonseca
(1796–1890)

CHAPTER 3

VASCO DA
Gama

Vasco da Gama was a Portuguese navigator and explorer. In addition to gaining much knowledge about the people and cultures of East Africa and India, he was the first person to sail from Europe to India. Da Gama helped open direct trade between Portugal and India. He also served as an advisor to Portugal's king on matters relating to India.

Vasco da Gama's signature

FAST FACTS

BIRTH DATE:
CIRCA 1460

PLACE OF BIRTH:
SINES, PORTUGAL

AGE AT DEATH:
ABOUT 64, DIED 1524

FAMOUS ACCOMPLISHMENT:
FINDING A MARITIME ROUTE TO INDIA

Da Gama's Youth

Many details about Vasco da Gama's early life remain unknown. We do know that he was born into a noble family around the year 1460, though some sources put the year of his birth as late as 1469. He was the third son born in his family.

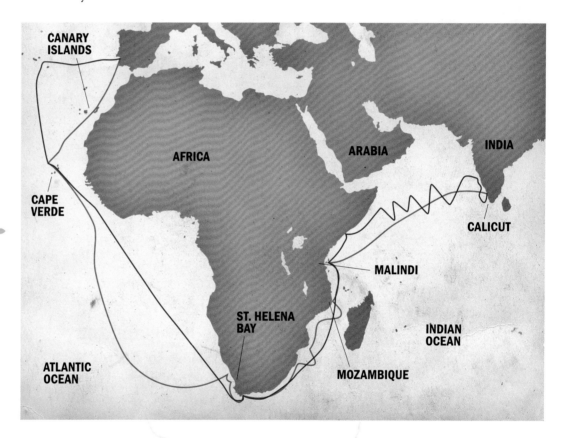

Da Gama's path of exploration

The blue line is his journey out and the red line is his journey homeward.

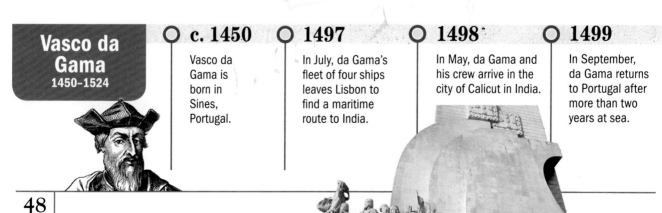

Vasco da Gama
1450–1524

c. 1450
Vasco da Gama is born in Sines, Portugal.

1497
In July, da Gama's fleet of four ships leaves Lisbon to find a maritime route to India.

1498
In May, da Gama and his crew arrive in the city of Calicut in India.

1499
In September, da Gama returns to Portugal after more than two years at sea.

Some say that da Gama's father, Estêvão da Gama, commanded a fortress in Sines, located in southwestern Portugal. Others say he was a knight.

No matter what his father's job was, Vasco da Gama probably received a good education. Why? His family came from the noble class. And since he lived near a seaport town, he probably learned about both ships and navigation.

Da Gama may have attended school in Évora, a village about 70 miles from Sines. By some accounts, he studied advanced math and navigation principles. As a teenager, he would also have become familiar with the different trading ships docked in the local port.

When did da Gama first serve as the captain of a ship? Some say he was just 20 years old! But much lay ahead in his future maritime adventures . . . .

A street sign for Alley of Vasco da Gama, in the Areias de São João of Albufeira, Algarve, Portugal

credit: Kolforn (CC BY 3.0)

"I am not the man I once was. I do not want to go back in time, to be the second son, the second man."

VASCO DA GAMA

1502

Da Gama is named Admiral of India by Portugal's king.

Da Gama returns to India. He makes trade agreements with the local people.

1503

Da Gama comes back to Portugal. He spends the next two decades with his family in his homeland.

1524

He is nominated as the Portuguese viceroy in India.

December 1524

Da Gama dies of illness in India.

A Job for the King

Even as a young man, da Gama was a skilled navigator. His reputation must have been impressive , because the Portuguese king, John II, put him in charge of a special mission in 1492.

French ships had been attacking Portuguese shipping interests. King John II was mad—he was not about to let another nation threaten Portuguese trade.

The king sent da Gama to Setúbal, a thriving port town. According to historian Garcia de Resende (1470–1536), King John II sent da Gama there "in a great hurry, with great provisions and powers."

Da Gama was successful in his mission. He retaliated against France by seizing several French vessels at Setúbal and in some ports of the Algarve, an area of Portugal.

 An illustration from an 1880 edition of *Os Lusiadas*

CONNECT

Learn more about Vasco da Gama in this video. Why were his explorations so important?

🔍 **Vasco da Gama history video**

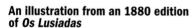

> "I am not afraid of the darkness.
> Real death is preferable to
> a life without living."
>
> **VASCO DA GAMA**

Portrait of King Manuel I
By Henrique Ferreira, 1720

Expedition East

The year 1497 was an important one for Vasco da Gama. The new Portuguese king, Manuel I, chose him to lead a Portuguese fleet of ships to India. The hope was that da Gama would finally complete what had originally been the goal of Bartolomeu Dias's expedition—to find a trading route to India.

While Dias had confirmed that the Atlantic and Indian Oceans were connected, he did not reach India as Portugal's leaders had hoped. Portugal's king was eager to claim faraway riches and land for his country.

Getting Ready

The Portuguese government didn't skimp when preparing for da Gama's expedition. Bartolomeu Dias made sure that da Gama's ships had the best navigational charts and up-to-date equipment.

They also had many firearms and cannons. After all, sailors never knew when they might need to fight off enemies.

Among da Gama's supplies were dried beef and wine, both of which could last for a long time. Da Gama's ships also carried many trinkets. Why? To trade for other goods with the indigenous peoples they met during their journey.

The Journey Begins

Da Gama's fleet of four vessels set sail from Lisbon on July 8, 1497. Da Gama sailed on the *São Gabriel*. And his younger brother, Paulo, headed the crew of the *São Rafael*. It must have been nice to have a family member during the long journey. Overall, the crew consisted of 170 men.

Bartolomeu Dias accompanied da Gama for part of this voyage. He provided expert advice on how to navigate down the West African coast and also served as pilot while the expedition made its way to the Canary Islands.

Dias continued acting as pilot until late July when they arrived at the Cape Verde islands, off the coast of present-day Senegal. Here, da Gama and Dias parted ways. Do you think Dias was disappointed to leave such a well-funded and well-equipped expedition?

An antique brass astrolabe

NAVIGATIONAL TOOLS USED ON DA GAMA'S EXPEDITION

Modern ships have all kinds of amazing technology, such as GPS and sonar. But that wasn't the case back when Vasco da Gama was sailing. In those days, a compass was one tool used to guide ships. Another tool was the astrolabe, which navigators began using in the 1400s. An astrolabe is a device used to determine latitude. Navigators used astrolabes to measure both the position of the sun as well as other objects in the sky, such as the North Star. By measuring the position of the stars and sun above the horizon, navigators could determine their latitude—how far north or south of the equator they were. These clever tools also helped navigators to estimate time.

Dias knew that storms and unpredictable winds were common in the area around the Gulf of Guinea. People often refer to this phenomenon as the doldrums. Dias advised da Gama's fleet to try something different. So they sailed away from the coastline and into the South Atlantic.

This new course took advantage of both the ocean currents and tradewinds to gain speed. Da Gama's fleet was 600 miles from Brazil before southwesterly tradewinds blew the ships back in the direction of southern Africa.

Even though the journey was longer in distance, it was speedier and easier than traveling close to Africa's west coast. This route is pretty much the same as the one used by ships sailing from Europe to India today.

Making Headway

Da Gama's fleet had not seen land for 13 weeks when they finally landed at St. Helena Bay in South Africa on November 7. That's a lot longer than the time Christopher Columbus (1436–1506) was out of sight of land during his famous trans-Atlantic journey. By the time da Gama reached St. Helena Bay, his crew had traveled more than 4,500 miles from the Cape Verde islands.

The west coast of Africa as it looks today in Ghana

CONNECT

You can look at the journal from Vasco da Gama's first voyage. Why are primary source documents such as these important?

🔍 **Da Gama journal first voyage**

SCURVY AND SAILORS

Luís de Camões, circa 1916
By George J Hagar (1847–1921)

Da Gama's expedition next headed around the Cape of Good Hope. They anchored their ships at Mossel Bay. Here, they traded with the local people. The sailors exchanged trinkets for an ox. Was this a fair trade? It's hard to say today whether both sides felt they got a good deal.

Not all da Gama's ships were in great shape by the time they arrived at Mossel Bay. The 200-ton storeship named *Berrio* was in especially poor condition. So da Gama ordered that it be broken up and burned—after shifting its contents to his other ships, of course!

Vasco da Gama's three remaining ships kept traveling north along the east coast of modern-day South Africa. The expedition continued sailing up Africa's eastern coast until they arrived at the River of Good Omens. They stayed here for about a month. Many crew members were sick with a disease called scurvy. Eventually, they headed back out to sea.

Scurvy is a disease that, in the past, often affected sailors at sea. It is caused by a lack of vitamin C, one of the nutrients our bodies need to function properly. People suffering from scurvy feel weak and very tired. They can have severe joint or leg pain. Their gums swell up and bleed—sometimes their teeth even fall out. And their skin bruises easily. It's very uncomfortable. Scurvy became more common among sailors as ships were able to stay out at sea longer. Luís de Camões (c. 1524–1580) was a poet and soldier who traveled on da Gama's voyage. He wrote a poem about death from scurvy.

"A dread disease its rankling horror shed,
  And death's dire ravage through mine army spread
  Never mind eyes such dreary sight beheld,
  Ghastly the mouth and gums enormous swell'd . . . ."

Trading Troubles and Incredible India

On March 2, 1498, da Gama's fleet arrived at the port of Mozambique. Da Gama hoped to trade with the ruling sultan there. But the sultan was not impressed with the goods da Gama had to offer.

The Portuguese explorers on this expedition had underestimated the high quality of goods being traded in Mozambique—gold, pearls, cotton, and ivory. Da Gama's team moved on.

CONNECT

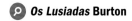

Portuguese poet Luís de Camões wrote an epic poem about Vasco da Gama and the discovery of a sea route from Portugal to India. Some of the long poem was narrated by the explorer. You can read parts of the poem translated into English at this website. Do you think poetry is a good way to describe a sea journey? Why or why not?

🔍 *Os Lusiadas* Burton

WONDER WHY?

Why are some goods valued more in some parts of the world than others? What decides the value of something?

At Malindi, located in modern-day Kenya, da Gama's fleet stopped again. Here, the captain hired a knowledgeable pilot. Going into uncharted territory, he hoped the pilot would help navigate the fleet as it made its way through the Indian Ocean.

Some say this pilot may have been the renowned Arab navigator named Ahmed Ibn Majid (1421–c. 1500) Others say he was a navigator from India.

After sailing for nearly four weeks, da Gama and his crew made it to the city of Calicut in May 1498. They had achieved the goal of reaching India by sea. This was huge news!

> "To discover the sea route to India, he deliberately set his course in a different direction from Columbus, his great seafaring rival."
>
> WRITER ERIC ORMSBY (1941–)

India's Malabar Coast was an essential center for spices in da Gama's time. In addition to having its own spices grown there, especially pepper, ships from Indonesia's Spice Islands came here to trade with Arab merchants from the Persian Gulf and Red Sea.

Da Gama's team stayed here for three months or so. At first, they were well-received by the area's Hindu ruler. But the Arab traders did not want to give up their control over the spice trade to Christians, including da Gama. Tensions grew. Da Gama's men barely managed to barter for the goods they needed for their journey home.

Tough Times, Then Homecoming

The trip back to Malindi was dreadful. Da Gama's team couldn't locate the pilot who'd helped them reach India, so they weren't as sure of their direction as they wanted to be. Monsoons made the voyage even more difficult and slow. It took three months to travel just 2,300 miles. Many of the crew suffered from scurvy, and 30 men died.

WONDER WHY?

On his first voyage to India, Vasco da Gama's profits were 6,000 percent. Talk about a return on investment! Do you think his expedition would be considered a success today, considering the number of deaths?

Luckily, the sultan of Malindi was a kind man. He took pity on da Gama's team and provided oranges and fresh meat for the men, saving many lives in the process. But even with the sultan's help, too few men were left alive to sail all three ships back to Portugal. This time, the *São Rafael* was burned.

CONNECT

Scientists and archaeologists have found what they believe to be the shipwreck of the *Esmeralda*, one of the ships on da Gama's fleet. You can see underwater footage and read about the site here.

🔍 *Esmeralda* shipwreck

The Monument to the Discoveries in Lisbon. Da Gama is third from the front.

On March 20, 1499, da Gama's remaining men sailed around the Cape of Good Hope. They arrived back in Lisbon six months later, on September 18.

Da Gama and his crew had been traveling for more than two years and had covered 24,000 miles. Even though only 54 of the expedition's original 170 men came back alive, King Manuel was delighted with the expedition's achievements.

Home and Away Again

Right after da Gama's successful return, the king decided to send off another expedition to set up a trading post at Calicut. Pedro Álvares Cabral led this fleet and made it to Calicut in less than six months.

In 1502, da Gama sailed back to India. His goal was to ensure that Portugal was dominant in this area. He left Lisbon with a fleet of 20 armed ships.

Explorers of this period wanted to take over as much land as they could from the people who already lived there. This is called colonization, and it has been a driving force in history since people first began to travel extensively.

To this end, da Gama behaved brutally toward Muslims on this expedition. The Portuguese had long battled Muslim Moors from North Africa for control of land in Portugal. This may explain why he treated Muslims so violently, attacking any Arab Muslim ships he encountered along the way.

WONDER WHY?

Vasco da Gama often acted in a brutal way when interacting with people involved with the Muslim shipping trade. How do you think explorers should interact with people they meet in their travels? What would you want to share from your own culture when arriving in a new place?

TRAVELING ACTRESSES

While few Renaissance women traveled far from home, during the sixteenth century, the earliest professional actresses in Italy emerged as part of traveling theater troupes. Some star actresses got to travel widely and in style. These talented women spread Italian methods of acting and productions called masks—a party of guests wearing costumes and masks—farther and farther afield. In the late 1560s, they made a splash in the European cities of Linz, Vienna, and Prague. Paris, Antwerp, Madrid, and London followed in the 1570s. The highly successful Italian actresses saw the globe and in the process served as cultural ambassadors.

In one especially cruel episode, da Gama ordered the killing of 380 people—including children and women—aboard a Muslim ship coming back from Mecca. When da Gama made it to Calicut, he continued his violent ways, destroying the Muslim trading post there and killing 38 hostages.

He also continued to establish Portugal's role as a very important spice trader in the region. He departed from the port of Cochin in February 1503. During his return journey, da Gama traveled up the east African coast and established some Portuguese trading posts in the area now known as Mozambique.

A 1524 painting of
Vasco da Gama

By Gregorio Lopes
(1490–1550)

Advisor to the King and a Last Voyage

After yet another successful voyage to India, Vasco da Gama continued to serve as advisor to the Portuguese king on matters related to India. He lived with his family in Portugal for the better part of two decades. Da Gama had a wife named Catarina de Ataíde. He also had a daughter and six sons.

In 1524, da Gama was nominated to be the Portuguese viceroy in India. A viceroy is a person who rules a province or country as the representative of his king or sovereign.

As viceroy, da Gama served as the Portuguese king's representative in India. He had the power to act in the king's name. One of his major tasks was to deal with the growing corruption among the Portuguese authorities stationed in India.

Da Gama made it to Cochin but soon got sick. He died on December 24, 1524. Fifteen years later, his body was brought back to Portugal to be buried.

What Makes Him Different?

Vasco da Gama is different from other Renaissance explorers in several ways. To begin with, he made more than one successful trip to India. He returned twice more to the subcontinent.

Perhaps the most striking difference between da Gama and other explorers of this era concerns his behavior.

ABUBAKARI II

Abubakari II was a powerful African man. During the fourteenth century, he ruled over a huge empire that covered almost all of West Africa. But Abubakari wasn't satisfied with just power and riches. He wanted to explore. In 1311, he did something radical—he gave his throne to his brother, Kankou Moussa. Then, he set off on his own expedition. Some scholars say he departed from what is now the country of Gambia with a fleet of 2,000 boats. They say that Abubakari II arrived on the coast of Brazil in 1312—beating Christopher Columbus to America by nearly two centuries!

While quite a few European explorers were not kind or fair toward the new peoples, and many were violent toward them, da Gama was especially brutal. The acts of violence that da Gama displayed toward the Muslim people he encountered during his voyages of discovery were shocking.

From ordering the massacre of Muslim pilgrims returning from Mecca to the gruesome capturing and killing of fishermen in India, Vasco da Gama showed terrible cruelty. He was both feared and hated by many.

Lasting Legacy

Vasco da Gama was the first European to reach India by sea. He opened an ocean-based trade route to the Indian subcontinent. He and his crew met and interacted with the peoples of many different lands and cultures, from the Cape Verde Islands to Mozambique.

The sea route that da Gama established gave Portugal the opportunity to set up a rich trade network with India and Southeast Asia. He finally succeeded in breaking the grip that the Arab and Venetian spice traders had on the area.

Da Gama's new route also allowed Portugal to expand its own empire through the addition of provinces in India and beyond.

A pillar of Vasco da Gama in eastern Africa

WORDS OF WONDER

What vocabulary words did you discover? Can you figure out the meanings of these words by using the context and roots? Look in the glossary for help!

doldrums · monsoon · latitude
barter · scurvy · trinket

Make a Marker

Many European explorers, including Vasco da Gama, left markers to indicate places they had reached on their voyages of exploration. The padrãos set up by Portuguese explorers were stone crosses. But what if you were traveling across the world on an expedition today? What kind of a creative landmark would you design and build?

> ➤ **Draw a sketch of what you'd like your marker to look like.** Keep in mind the goals of your imaginary expedition as well as the places you might be visiting.

> ➤ **Brainstorm the kind of materials you'd like to use for your marker.** Cardboard, wood, recycled containers, papier mâché—what can you think of to use for your memorial?

> ➤ **Assemble the materials to create your marker.** How tall do you want it to be? Will it be colorful or just one shade—such as a gray slab of stone?

> ➤ **Build your marker until you are satisfied with it.**

> ➤ **If you have permission and space to do so, connect your marker to a garden stake.** Gently place the marker into the soil. You have left your mark on the landscape!

Think About It!

> ➤ **How do you think someone would react if you placed your marker on their front lawn without permission?** Do you think this might be similar to the reaction of indigenous people when explorers left their stone crosses on beaches and cliffs? Do you think explorers ever considered this? Why or why not?

Create an Hourglass

In the days before explorers had watches, other methods were used to keep time. Da Gama's crew used hourglasses—large for 1 hour, smaller for 30 minutes—to keep time during their voyage. In this activity, you'll make your own hourglass.

> ➤ **Using the funnel, pour sand into one of the bottles.** Fill it about two-thirds full.

> ➤ **Carefully, with the help of an adult, use the hammer and nail to poke one hole in the plastic bottle cap.**

> ➤ **Place this cap onto the top of the bottle filled with sand.**

> ➤ **Tip the empty drink bottle upside down.** Place it on top of the sand-filled bottle. Secure the two bottles together using duct tape.

> ➤ **Flip over the bottles so the sand starts flowing through.** Use a stopwatch to see how long it takes all the sand to flow from one bottle into the other.

Try This!

> ➤ **Can you make an "hourglass" that lasts for 30 minutes?** How might you adjust your materials to change the amount of time you're measuring? Is there a way to do it without using trial and error?

PÊRO DA COVILHÃ

A bronze medal with an image of Pêro da Covilhã

CHAPTER 4

PÊRO DA Covilhã

Pêro da Covilhã was a Portuguese adventurer and explorer. He carried out several diplomatic missions for Portugal in various North African and European countries. He explored the trade routes that linked the Mediterranean Sea with the Indian Ocean. Da Covilhã also established relations between Portugal and Abyssinia, now called Ethiopia.

Detail of monument showing Pêro da Covilhã

credit: Pedro Nuno Caetano (CC BY 2.0)

FAST FACTS

BIRTH DATE:
C. 1460

PLACE OF BIRTH:
COVILHÃ, PORTUGAL

AGE AT DEATH:
BETWEEN 66 AND 70, DIED BETWEEN 1526 AND 1530

FAMOUS ACCOMPLISHMENT:
ONE OF THE FIRST PORTUGUESE EXPLORERS OF AFRICA WHO ESTABLISHED RELATIONS BETWEEN PORTUGAL AND ETHIOPIA

Pêro Da Covilhã's Early Life

Da Covilhã was born around 1460 in Covilhã, a small city in eastern Portugal. While historians know few details about da Covilhã's earliest years, they do know some things about how the young boy spent his time. (Does this sound familiar? This is similar to many of the explorers we've discussed in this book!)

The city of Covilhã today

credit: Feliciano Guimarães (CC BY 2.0)

Pêro da Covilhã 1460–1530	c. 1460	1476	1480s	1487
	Da Covilhã is born in Covilhã, Portugal.	Da Covilhã takes part in the Battle of Toro.	He serves as a messenger and spy for the Portuguese king on missions to Spain and North Africa.	Da Covilhã and Afonso de Paiva leave Portugal to try to reach India and Ethiopia.

When he was just six years old, young da Covilhã started serving as a page in the duke of Medina-Sidonia's household in Seville, Spain. He stayed in this position until he was a teenager. It is said that da Covilhã was a quick, clever, and trustworthy boy.

In late 1474 or early 1475, da Covilhã went back to Portugal with the duke's brother. At this point, he changed jobs. He started working in the service of the royal court, located in Lisbon. He served as a junior squire to Portugal's King Afonso V (1432–1481). This was a prestigious position for a young man. It also offered the potential for good jobs in the future.

Traveling with the King

As part of his work serving the king, da Covilhã had the chance to travel more than the average teenager. He journeyed to Plasencia in Spain with Afonso V when Afonso claimed the title of king of Castile. While today this journey would take just a few hours by car, in the days before cars, trains, or planes, such a trip took much longer.

✦ THE LIFE OF A SQUIRE ✦

Pêro da Covilhã spent much of his childhood and teenaged years in the service of nobles. One job was as a squire. Squires were typically around 14 years old or so. They had already served for several years as pages before becoming squires. Squires had to learn many different skills. These skills included horsemanship and how to use a variety of weapons. Squires had to develop athletic skills, such as climbing and swimming. Why? One never knew when a castle might come under siege. In addition to physical strength and skills, squires were educated in the code of chivalry. They learned to dance and behave according to courtly rules of etiquette. Being a squire was hard work and required mastering many challenging skills!

1488
Da Covilhã reaches the city of Aden on the Red Sea.

1488
He arrives on the Malabar Coast of India.

1490–1
He reaches Cairo, Egypt, and discovers that Afonso de Paiva has died.

1493–4
Da Covilhã arrives in Ethiopia.

1526–30
Da Covilhã dies in Ethiopia.

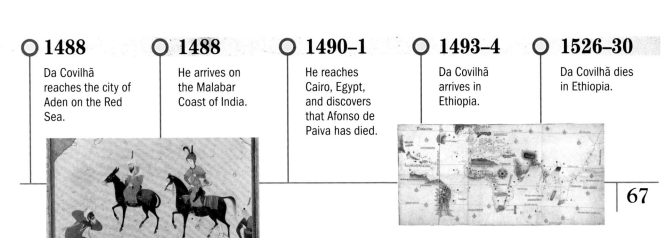

King Afonso V of Portugal in a hand-colored sketch from the journal of Georg von Ehingen (1428-1508)

"One would like to think that it was da Covilhã's values that were instrumental in bringing Portugal and Ethiopia together as equals, the one accepting of the other."

AUTHOR JOHN JEREMY HESPELER-BOULTBEE (1935–)

In March 1476, da Covilhã took part in the Battle of Toro. Toro was a town in Spain, located just a few miles from the Duero River. This battle was between the king of Spain, known as Fernando the Catholic (1452–1516), and King Afonso V of Portugal. Portugal's king was defeated in this battle.

After this defeat, da Covilhã also accompanied King Afonso V on a trip to France. They returned to Portugal in November 1477.

Secret Messages and Missions to North Africa

After King Afonso V died in 1481, da Covilhã worked for his son, King John II. He served as a squire of Portugal's royal guard. He also worked as a messenger, conveying confidential messages to Spain. King John II chose da Covilhã to take on important diplomatic missions to North Africa.

The hero Duarte de Almeida holds the Portuguese royal standard during the Battle of Toro (1476)

By José Bastos, circa 1900. The Battle of Toro is known for not being completely decisive. Both sides claimed victory, though history shows that the outcome was worse for Portugal.

ISABELLA D'ESTE

Portrait of Isabella d'Este

By Leonardo da Vinci, circa 1499–1500

When reading of Renaissance expeditions, all the patrons of these voyages seem to be men. Likewise, when explorers such as da Covilhã met up with leaders from other nations, they were also men. Weren't there any female leaders back then?

Yes, but not very many. One such leader was a woman named Isabella d'Este (1474–1539). D'Este was part of the ruling family of Ferrara in Italy. She married a man named Francesco Gonzaga (1466–1519), who happened to be a prince.

When d'Este's husband died, she ruled the northern Italian city of Mantua—on her own. She demonstrated fantastic leadership skills as Mantua's chief of state. D'Este founded a school for young women at a time when most girls stayed home and learned domestic skills such as cooking and taking care of children. D'Este also collected art, such as statues and paintings. She wrote letters on topics ranging from war to politics. She showed the world that women could do the same jobs as men—and just as well!

On one such mission da Covilhã was given orders to bring messages of peace to the northwestern African people called the Moors. Da Covilhã also hoped to befriend the ruler of Tlemcen while traveling. Today, Tlemcen is a city located in northwestern Algeria near the border with Morocco.

Tlemcen was a cultural and religious center of Islam. It also was an essential place in the trading routes along northern Africa's coast.

Textile making was a vital part of the industry here. Da Covilhã had been asked to help Portugal gain a trading monopoly over valuable carpet production in the region.

> "Master Leonardo—Hearing that you are staying in Florence, we have conceived the hope that something we have long desired might come true: to have something by your hand."
>
> **FROM A LETTER BY ISABELLA D'ESTE TO LEONARDO DA VINCI**

Big Goals and Exciting Explorations

By 1487, da Covilhã had certainly earned the trust of King John II. He had successfully completed several diplomatic missions and conveyed secret messages in a variety of locations. Da Covilhã was not only a clever adventurer, he was also fluent in Arabic and several other languages.

King John II was interested in making money from the spice trade in India. He also wanted to reach out to connect with Prester John, the Christian leader of Abyssinia (now called Ethiopia). The king hoped that perhaps Portugal could form an alliance with this legendary leader. You can learn more about Prester John on page 35.

Da Covilhã was selected by King John II to participate in a new exploratory mission to India. He traveled with a squire named Afonso de Paiva (dates unknown), who also spoke Arabic.

The two departed Portugal in May 1487. Their route took them through Barcelona and then by boat to Naples and Rhodes, an island off the coast of present-day Turkey.

WONDER WHY?

We know that Pêro da Covilhã spoke Arabic in addition to Portuguese. How does knowing the language of the local people benefit an explorer? Do you know more than one language? How might that help you in the future?

IBN BATTUTA

An illustration of Ibn Battuta from Jules Verne's book *Découverte de la terre (Discovery of the Earth)*, drawn by Léon Benett

Pêro da Covilhã traveled to Morocco on one of his early missions for the king of Portugal. But did you know that one of the world's most famous explorers came from Morocco? Many historians consider Ibn Battuta (1304–1377) to be "the greatest traveler of all time."

Born in Tangiers, Morocco, Ibn Battuta was an Islamic scholar. Between 1325 and 1354, Battuta traveled 75,000 miles through more than 40 different countries in the Middle East, Africa, and Asia. That's more than four times the distance traveled by Marco Polo (1254–1324)!

During his travels, Battuta met with well-known religious figures, famous rulers, and Muslim intellectuals. Sometimes, this adventurer served as a diplomat. Other times, he acted as a pilgrim or a politician. He opened the world up for many through his book, *Travels in Asia and Africa 1325–1354*.

It was on Rhodes that da Covilhã and his fellow travel companion disguised themselves as honey merchants and continued by ship to Alexandria, Egypt. Even the best made plans sometimes fall apart. Both da Covilhã and de Paiva got sick.

They also had their goods taken away. Luckily, they were able to buy other items and travel on to Cairo, Egypt. Here they joined some North African people who were traveling to Aden, a port city located on the Gulf of Aden.

Da Covilhã and his travel companions arrived at the trade center of Aden during the summer of 1488. But at this point, Pêro da Covilhã and Afonso de Paiva went their separate ways. The two men were heading in different directions to try and accomplish the king's many objectives.

Da Covilhã would head toward India. De Paiva would try to establish contact with Prester John.

Adventures in India

Pêro da Covilhã headed out from Aden with the goal of reaching India. He sailed to India's Malabar coast, located on the western side of the subcontinent.

For many centuries, this area had been known for its spices and the spice trade. While on the Malabar coast, da Covilhã gained valuable information about the various ports in the area, such as Calicut.

One of his tasks was to explore and investigate India's spice ports. Da Covilhã quickly discovered that Calicut was not only the busiest of India's spice-trading cities, but also the most important.

The area surrounding this city had valuable orchards where pepper and ginger grew. Calicut's harbor was jam-packed with Chinese junks carrying cloves and cinnamon from lands farther east and with Arab dhows, too. It must have smelled amazing!

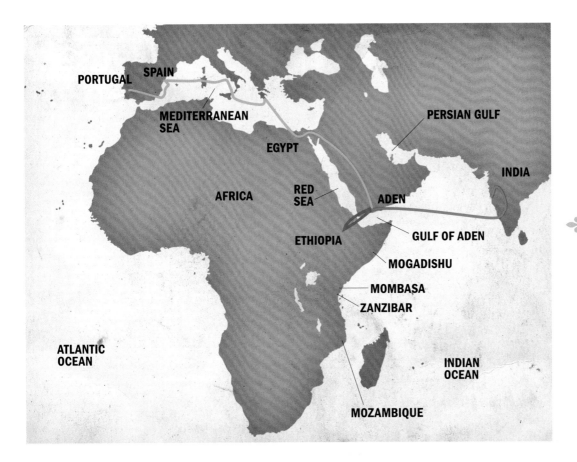

Da Covilhã's path of exploration

The light blue line is his journey out, the green is his path to India, and the dark blue is his venture to what is now Ethiopia.

CALECHVT CELEBERRI-
MVM INDIÆ EMPORIVM.

Calicut in 1572, from the Georg Braun and Franz Hogenbergs atlas, *Civitates Orbis Terrarum*

Sad News

Sometime between October 1489 and March 1490, da Covilhã traveled to Ormuz, located in Persia. Ormuz was an island fortress in the Persian Gulf.

Here, the explorer learned about an overland trade route to the Mediterranean Sea, which took travelers by way of Basra at the head of the Persian Gulf. This route provided an alternative to the water route over the Red Sea.

CONNECT

Learn more about the Portuguese fort at Ormuz.

🔍 **Ormuz wdl**

From Ormuz, da Covilhã traveled by sea to the coast of East Africa. Along the way, he made stops at the port cities of Mogadishu, Mombasa, and Zanzibar. Eventually, our adventurer made it to Mozambique. This was basically as far south as the Arab trade network went.

In Cairo, Egypt, da Covilhã learned that his former traveling companion, Afonso de Paiva, was dead. He also met up with messengers from King John II. They told da Covilhã that he could return to Portugal with honor. But only if he had completed the exploratory missions in both India and Ethiopia.

Da Covilhã wrote a long report to the king telling him all about his experiences on the journey up to that point.

Arrival in Ethiopia—the Land of No Return

Da Covilhã was determined to make his way to Ethiopia. He headed to Ormuz, along with one of the Portuguese messengers he'd met in Cairo. From there, the explorer journeyed to the Red Sea. Why? He was looking for a good way to approach the land of Ethiopia.

In order to blend in and stay safe during his travels in the region, da Covilhã disguised himself as a Muslim man. In this disguise, he visited the holy cities of Medina and Mecca. Some sources say that he was the first known European to visit Mecca, the holiest city in Islam.

WONDER WHY?

We don't know whether the report Pêro da Covilhã wrote about his travels ever made it back to Portugal's king. What might have happened to it? If it did reach Portugal, what benefits might it have had for future explorers?

Da Covilhã also visited Mount Sinai. Sometime in 1492 or 1493, he reached the city of Zeila, now in Somalia. From here, he traveled by caravan to his final destination of Ethiopia. Historians believed that he arrived in Ethiopia either late in 1493 or early in 1494.

The ruler of Ethiopia, known as Emperor Eskender (1471–1494), gave da Covilhã a courteous welcome to his Christian nation. The Portuguese explorer was treated very well.

Map of the East African coast, circa 1500

By George McCall Theal, 1902, *The Beginning of South African History*

Muslim Pilgrim to Mecca Meets a Brahman on the Road

By Amir Khusrau Dihlavi

Pêro da Covilhã was wildly successful in his goals of reaching India and Ethiopia. But everything was not perfect. The emperor forbade da Covilhã from leaving the country. The explorer had landed in the place where he would live out the rest of his life. Pêro da Covilhã died in Ethiopia sometime between the years 1526 and 1530.

DIPLOMACY

Even though da Covilhã was stuck in Ethiopia, relations were established between Portugal and Ethiopia. Years after his arrival there, the Ethiopian government sent a messenger to Portugal. The messenger arrived in 1514. After this connection was made, a Portuguese embassy was sent to Ethiopia. In December 1520, the Portuguese ambassador met up with da Covilhã. The adventurer was old but healthy. He served as both an interpreter and a guide for the Portuguese and Ethiopian parties.

Da Covilhã's needs were generously provided for. He was even given a wife! In addition, the Portuguese adventurer was given an important place in the Ethiopian court. He became the governor of a district in this far-off land.

What Makes Him Different?

Pêro da Covilhã had an interesting background. Before he became an explorer, da Covilhã served as a spy for King John II.

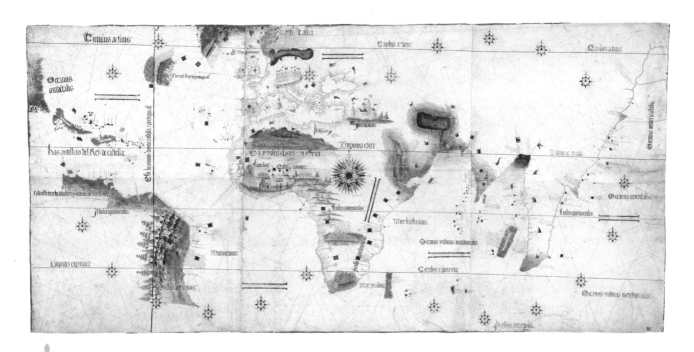

The Cantino planisphere, completed by an unknown Portuguese cartographer in 1502, shows what people thought the world looked like during the Age of Exploration in the beginning of the sixteenth century.

Lasting Legacy

Pêro da Covilhã played an important role in Portugal's era of exploration. He gathered much information about the lands and peoples he encountered on his journey from Portugal to India, as well as on his mission to Ethiopia. He also gained knowledge about the extent and activity of the spice trade, especially on India's Malabar coast.

While other Portuguese explorers such as Vasco da Gama were very biased against many of the foreign people they came across, da Covilhã was not. For example, he came to Ethiopia with an open mind. He even became an honored member of the court of the Ethiopian emperor.

Da Covilhã was the first European to reach the Ethiopian court. He was instrumental in helping establish friendly relations in 1520 with the country now called Ethiopia.

WORDS OF WONDER

What vocabulary words did you discover? Can you figure out the meanings of these words by using the context and roots? Look in the glossary for help!

**ambassador · biased · diplomatic
values · monopoly · prestigious**

77

Project

Try Some Ethiopian Food

What You Need

¼ cup teff flour, ¾ cup all-purpose flour, 1 cup water, a pinch (about ⅛ teaspoon) salt, vegetable or peanut oil

Explorers such as Pêro da Covilhã probably tried lots of new foods during their travels. Since he lived for a long time in Ethiopia, da Covilhã probably ate *injera*, a type of flatbread commonly eaten there. This bread has a bubbly, airy texture and a slightly sour taste. **You will need an adult to help with the actual cooking.**

➤ **Put the teff flour into a mixing bowl.** Gradually stir in the all-purpose flour. Add the water, a little at a time. Stir it so you can avoid lumps in the batter.

➤ **Let the batter sit for at least one full day (but up to three days is fine).** This allows the *injera* to ferment. The batter will begin to bubble. That's okay! The bubbling means that the bread will gain the tangy taste it's known for. If for some reason your batter doesn't bubble, add a teaspoon of yeast and leave it to bubble. Stir the salt into the batter.

➤ **Have an adult to help you with the rest of the recipe.** Heat either a nonstick pan or a slightly oiled cast iron pan on the stovetop. The pan is ready to use when a drop of water looks to be "dancing" on the pan's surface.

➤ **Lightly coat the pan with a thin layer of batter.** *Injera* batter is a little thinner than traditional pancake batter. As it heats up, the batter will rise a little.

➤ **Cook the *injera* until holes appear on the bread's surface.** When the top of the bread looks dry, take it out of the pan and let it cool.

WONDER WHY?

What would you have done if you arrived in a foreign country—as Pêro da Covilhã did in Ethiopia—and were told you could not go home? How do you think da Covilhã dealt with this situation?

Animals of Arabia

Pêro da Covilhã may have been the first European to visit Mecca and Medina. These cities are located in modern-day Saudi Arabia. Da Covilhã would have seen many different kinds of plants and animals in this area.

> ➤ **Using books and, with an adult's permission, the internet, research what kinds of plants and animals the explorer might have seen during his travels near Mecca and Medina.** For example, several types of acacia trees and shrubs grow here. Wild animals include mongooses and kangaroo rats, among others.

> ➤ **After you complete your research, create a poster, sculpture, or other artform of your choice.** Show the plants or animals you discovered and what they look like.

> ➤ **If you're inspired, make a diorama showing both the plants and animals found here.** Get creative!

Palm trees in Saudi Arabia

credit: haitham alfalah (public domain)

FERNAND, MAGELLAN

De, L'armessin, scul.

CHAPTER 5

FERDINAND
Magellan

Memorial to Ferdinand Magellan in Punta Arenas

credit: RAYANDBEE

Ferdinand Magellan was a Portuguese explorer and navigator. This brave seafarer sailed in the service of Spain and was the first European to cross the vast Pacific Ocean. Magellan was also an essential player in the first circumnavigation of the world. His expeditions showed clearly that all the world's oceans were connected.

FAST FACTS

BIRTH DATE:
C. 1480

PLACE OF BIRTH:
NORTHERN PORTUGAL

**AGE AT DEATH: 41,
DIED 1521**

FAMOUS ACCOMPLISHMENT:
HE LED THE FIRST EXPEDITION TO CIRCUMNAVIGATE THE GLOBE.

Magellan's Childhood

Historians are not sure exactly where and when Ferdinand Magellan was born. We do know that he was born in northern Portugal around 1480.

Magellan was born into a family that was part of the lower nobility. His father was the mayor of a town. Not much is known about his mother, though some sources mention that she also came from a noble family. Magellan had two siblings, a sister named Isabel and a brother named Diogo.

When Magellan was about 10 years old, his parents died. Luckily, his family had helpful connections. His grandmother on his father's side was part of the de Sousa family, a noble family that was thought highly of by the royal house in Portugal. What did that mean for young Magellan? Opportunity!

A sketch of Magellan, 1886

credit: Library of Congress

Ferdinand Magellan
1480–1521

c. 1480
Magellan is born in northern Portugal.

1490
Magellan's parents die, leaving him an orphan.

1490s
Magellan serves as a page in the Portuguese royal court in Lisbon. He remains part of the court for more than a decade.

1505
Magellan becomes a sailor in the fleet of Francisco de Almeida.

> "The sea is dangerous and its storms terrible, but these obstacles have never been sufficient reason to remain ashore . . . unlike the mediocre, intrepid spirits seek victory over those things that seem impossible . . . it is with an iron will that they embark on the most daring of all endeavors . . . to meet the shadowy future without fear and conquer the unknown."
>
> **FERDINAND MAGELLAN**

From the Royal Court to the High Seas

Young Magellan moved to Lisbon to become a page in the royal court. At this time, King John II and Queen Leonor were the highest members of the Portuguese royalty.

As a page, he would have been fed well and dressed in nice clothing. Pages worked as assistants to the royal family. Sometimes, they ran errands or attended royal functions. Pages needed to be familiar with proper court manners.

Being brought up in the Portuguese court, Magellan would have studied astronomy and nautical sciences, among other subjects. He would have had hints about how large the world really was. These studies gave Magellan a real enthusiasm for the voyages of discovery taking place at the time.

Magellan hoped to have his own adventures on the high seas. Eventually, he did . . . .

CONNECT

You can learn more about Magellan in this video!

🔍 **Magellan mini Bio**

1511
He is in Malacca when Portugal takes control of this territory.

1517
Magellan moves to Spain.

1519
Magellan's fleet departs Seville and heads west, hoping to circumnavigate the world.

1520
The fleet finds the water passage that will be known as the Strait of Magellan.

1521
Magellan dies during a battle in the Philippines.

1522
Juan Sebastian Elcano arrives back in Spain in the *Victoria*.

> "The Church says that the Earth is flat, but I know that it is round."
>
> **FERDINAND MAGELLAN**

THE TREATY OF TORDESILLAS

Portugal and Spain were huge rivals that both tried to claim new lands during their voyages of exploration. In 1494, a new treaty was made. It was called the Treaty of Tordesillas. According to the treaty, Spain and Portugal agreed upon an east-west division of the New World.

An imaginary line was created to divide the world so that any unclaimed territories to the west of the line would belong to Spain. Those to the east of the line would fall under Portugal's control. This treaty worked out nicely for both the Portuguese and Spanish empires, but not so well for the roughly 50 million people who already lived in previously established communities in the Americas.

Magellan thought that the Moluccas, or Spice Islands, would fall into Spain's portion of the world, according to the Treaty of Tordesillas.

Read more about the Treaty of Tordesillas at this website. How does this treaty still affect the world today?

🔍 **Nat Geo Treaty of Tordesillas**

First Sea Ventures

Magellan was a man who was not afraid to take risks or to create his own path to adventure and success. After many years as a page, he did something bold.

Magellan resigned from his position in the Portuguese court. Why? To become a seaman! Have you ever taken a risk like this before?

In 1505, Magellan set off for his first venture at sea. He was part of the fleet of Francisco de Almeida (1450–1510), the newly appointed viceroy of India. This fleet was the biggest to ever leave Lisbon. With 22 ships and nearly 2,000 men, this expedition must have seemed exciting to the young Magellan.

One goal of this expedition was to make sure that Portugal enforced its monopoly on trade in the area around the Cape of Good Hope. If Portugal let other countries get the advantage here, it would lose its thriving economic status. The expedition was also supposed to set up a series of fortified bases along the African coast.

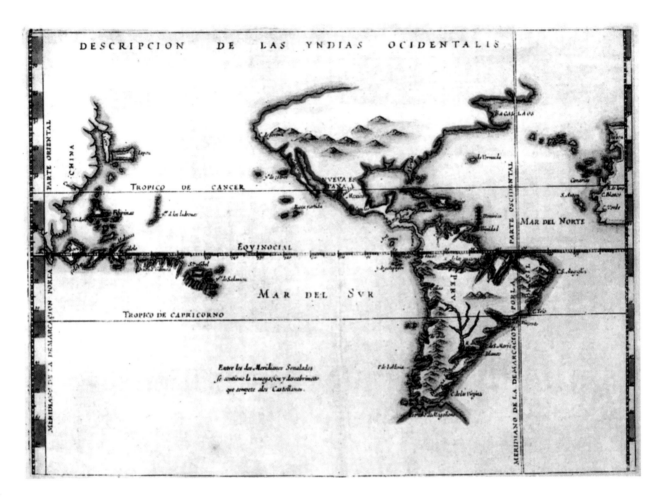

A map by Antonio de Herrera y Tordesillas (1559–1625) showing the east-west division of the New World

As Portugal tried to secure its control over trade with India, conflict was inevitable. A brave fighter, Magellan was wounded in a battle at Cannanore in India. He also was injured during another conflict on an island called Diu.

During the summer of 1511, Magellan found himself in the city of Melacca, in present-day Malaysia. Portugal successfully took over this city while Magellan was there, securing the country's dominance over India in trade.

While in Melacca, Magellan received letters that made him think about his future. The letters were from Francisco Serrão (died 1521), a Portuguese explorer who had visited the Moluccas east of Melacca. These islands were rich in spices, including cinnamon, pepper, cloves, and ginger.

Magellan was curious. Merchants could make a fortune selling such spices to willing and wealthy Europeans. Magellan wondered if he could get rich, too.

Bad Luck in Morocco

In 1512, Magellan returned to Portugal. He volunteered to join a Portuguese expedition headed to Morocco. He served his home country fighting people known as the Moors in the Battle of Azamor. It was during his time in Morocco that Magellan sustained a terrible knee injury. As a result, he walked with a limp for the rest of his life. As if being seriously wounded wasn't bad enough, Magellan was accused of a crime he didn't commit.

LET'S MAKE A DEAL

Explorers throughout the Age of Discovery wanted to see the world. Royal patrons hoped to control new lands and get rich through the establishment of new trade. For all parties involved in a Renaissance expedition, negotiations were necessary. Everyone wanted to come back from a voyage better off than they started.

Consider the example of Magellan's big expedition. He needed money to purchase ships and supplies for the journey. Spain's King Charles I provided the funds for these items. What did the king get in return for his financial support? A contract ensured that for 10 years, Spain's king would have control over any trade routes Magellan established. The king also would be entitled to "a fifth of the treasures found by Magellan's crew."

His peers claimed he had sold cattle to the enemy—the Moors. Even though Magellan didn't actually do this and the charge was dismissed, his reputation was damaged.

"Magellan's feat, by any measure—moral, intellectual, or physical—would excel even that of Gama or Columbus or Vespucci. He would face rougher seas, negotiate more treacherous passages and find his way across a broader ocean."

HISTORIAN DANIEL BOORSTIN (1914–2004)

An 1819 engraving of Magellan
credit: Library of Congress

Goodbye, Portugal

Magellan returned to Portugal after his time in Morocco. He asked Portugal's King Manuel I to fund an expedition to the Spice Islands—he was still thinking about getting rich. But the king wasn't very supportive of Magellan.

What could Magellan do without the king's support? He didn't have the money to fund his own expedition. But Magellan was no quitter. In a particularly brave move, he asked the king if he could look for support from another country. King Manuel I gave him permission to try elsewhere. So, in 1517, Magellan left his homeland and moved to Spain.

WONDER WHY?

Do you think Magellan showed disloyalty in going to Spain to try to find money for his voyage?

Establishing a Reputation

In October 1517, Magellan arrived in the Spanish city of Seville. What did he hope to achieve? Magellan wanted to go to the Moluccas. But he had a very unusual idea.

Magellan's plan was to sail west around South America to reach the Spice Islands. That was not what any previous explorers had done. Was such a thing even possible? Magellan was determined to find out. He enlisted the help of a friend named Rui Faleiro (dates unknown). Faleiro was a talented Portuguese mathematician and cosmographer.

Magellan hoped that Faleiro could help him provide scientific evidence to state that a southwest route from Europe to Asia was possible. Faleiro made false claims—he said that he could measure longitude accurately, which wasn't true. But Magellan also studied Francisco Serrão's account, which he hoped would help him work out the exact location of the Moluccas.

Longitude is the distance of a place east or west of the prime meridian, which is an imaginary line that runs from the North Pole to the South Pole. Knowing your longitude helps you to know where you are on the planet.

Magellan didn't know yet all the details for his dream expedition, but he had gathered enough information to impress others. Magellan also became a Spanish citizen. This probably helped prove his allegiance to his new home country.

WONDER WHY?

If you were an explorer today preparing for a voyage of discovery, what foods, supplies, and items to trade would you bring? Why did you choose these goods?

Magellan looked for a royal patron who could fund his dream expedition. He was given the chance to meet with Spain's King Charles I (1500–1558) and he managed to gain the king's support. On March 22, 1518, he signed a contract with the king.

Magellan was finally going to head his own fleet!

WHAT SUPPLIES DID MAGELLAN BRING ON HIS JOURNEY?

Packing for any trip requires planning. Renaissance explorers could never be sure how long they would be gone. Or how often they would get the chance to resupply. Whenever Magellan's fleet made landfall, it sought out fresh water and food. In addition to flour, water, dried meat, and cheese, the basic food supplies included the following items, among others:

- 200 barrels of anchovies
- 250 strings of garlic
- 7 cows
- 508 butts of wine
- 3 pigs

Magellan's ships also carried gunpowder, a variety of weapons, and navigational instruments. The explorer and his crew also brought other items to trade with local people. These items included mirrors, fishhooks, knives, brass bracelets, and about 20,000 small bells.

Prima ego velivolis ambivi cursibus Orbem,
Magellane novo te duce ducta freto.
Ambivi, meritoq3 vocor VICTORIA; sunt mî
Vela, alæ; precium, gloria; pugna, mare.

The Voyage Begins

On September 20, 1519, Magellan's fleet of five ships—known as the Armada de Molucca—set sail, heading west into the Atlantic Ocean. Magellan himself commanded the *Trinidad*, the fleet's flagship. The other ships were the *San Antonio, Santiago, Victoria*, and *Concepción*. How many men sailed with Magellan? Figures between 240 and 277 are most common. About three dozen of Magellan's crew members were Portuguese, but there were also members from Italy, other parts of Europe, and North Africa.

The expedition started off well. The fleet stopped for less than a week at the Canary Islands. Here, they repaired the ships and purchased additional supplies. By October 1519, the fleet had crossed the equator. Magellan's ships reached the coast of Brazil in December. Progress was being made!

A detail from a map by Abraham Ortelius (1527–1598) showing Magellan's ship, the *Victoria*

Trouble Brews

In December 1519, Magellan and his men spent nearly two weeks in Rio de Janeiro, located in present-day Brazil. The bay was beautiful, and the weather was nice.

Here, the fleet had a chance to resupply for the next stage of their journey. The native peoples were friendly. It must have been hard to leave what could have seemed like paradise.

Magellan ordered his crew to head south from Rio de Janeiro. The ships made their way along the coast of what are now Uruguay and Argentina. The ships faced roaring gales and treacherous coastlines. Storms damaged the fleet. And the temperature grew colder and colder as they sailed south.

WONDER WHY?

Magellan seemed to have a lot of problems with members of his crew during the course of his expedition. Can you think of ways that he could have made more positive connections with the other captains and crew members he traveled with?

> **"That caused the captain to fall face downward, when immediately they rushed upon him with iron and bamboo spears and with their cutlasses, until they killed our mirror, our light, our comfort, and our true guide."**
>
> **ANTONIO PIGAFETTA'S ACCOUNT OF MAGELLAN'S DEATH**

What was Magellan looking for as he headed so far south? He was searching for a water passage he hoped would lead to Asia.

But Magellan was known for being something of a dictator. He wouldn't tell the captains of the other ships in his fleet the exact route they were taking. The other ships had to stay close enough to use flag signals to remain in contact.

By the time Magellan's ships reached Port St. Julian in Patagonia, they clearly needed to stop. The winter weather was making it impossible to forge ahead. The men complained bitterly about having to stay in such a gloomy port. Even worse, their food supplies were running so low that the men had to survive on reduced rations.

Memorial to Ferdinand Magellan in Punta Arenas

credit: RAYANDBEE

On Easter Sunday, some of Magellan's men had had enough. Two of his captains led a mutiny against Magellan. However, not enough of the crew supported this act of rebellion.

Magellan quickly put down the mutiny. He ordered one of the rebel captains to be beheaded. The other was left behind on the coast.

CONNECT

You can watch a reenactment of Magellan's journey in this video!

🔍 **Magellan discovery BBC**

A Shipwreck and a Strait

Could things get any worse for Magellan's fleet? Unfortunately, yes. As the *Santiago* explored the southern coast of what today is Argentina, it ran aground. The ship was destroyed.

Eventually, Magellan had better luck. On October 21, 1520, he arrived at what turned out to be the opening to the passage he'd been looking for. Today, it's known as the Strait of Magellan. The passage winds its way through the tip of South America, giving ships a way between the Atlantic and Pacific Oceans without have to round the tip out in the open ocean. It took the fleet a grueling 38 days to make its way through the 334-mile-long strait.

Strait of Magellan

Sometime during the early navigation of the strait, the *San Antonio* deserted the expedition, taking its men and provisions with it. The ship headed back to Spain.

In November, Magellan and his three remaining ships entered a calm ocean lit by a lovely golden sunset. Many sources say that Magellan wept at this site. It was Magellan who gave this vast ocean its name, the Pacific.

One Vast Ocean

As Magellan's fleet headed north into the open Pacific, he believed that the Moluccas were just a short distance away. Perhaps just a few days. He couldn't have been more wrong. Magellan's fleet did not reach the Spice Islands in a matter of days . . . or even weeks.

Months passed and still the ships didn't come across any inhabited islands. An Italian man named Antonio Pigafetta (1480–1534) served as an assistant to Magellan and kept a journal of the voyage. He described how desperate the situation had grown, "We [had] passed three months and twenty days without obtaining any provisions, eating powdered biscuit, riddled with worms . . . rats were sold for half a ducat each, and even they could not be got."

The men even resorted to soaking leather in salt water and roasting it to eat!

Many members of Magellan's expedition died of scurvy or malnutrition. Sharks followed the ships, eating their fill of the corpses that were thrown overboard. It was grim. Finally, things began to look up. On March 6, 1521, Magellan's fleet arrived at the Mariana Islands.

Engraving from 1598 from
Effigies Regum ac Principum
By Crispijn van de Passe the Elder

Getting fresh food and water must have been thrilling to Magellan's starving crew. But the local islanders came aboard the ships and took equipment. Magellan's men, in their weakened condition, weren't up for a fight. They just watched their possessions disappear. Magellan referred to the island as the Island of Thieves.

Why did the islanders steal Magellan's things? It was not because they were bad. Instead, the people living here had a different idea of property rights. They shared their possessions. But Magellan's team did not know that at the time.

Sailing West— Another Tragedy

After a few days in the Marianas, Magellan's fleet headed west. He made it to the Philippines by mid-March. On an island called Cebu, Magellan became friends with a ruler. He persuaded this man to convert to Christianity.

Just weeks later, Magellan made a terrible mistake when he got involved in a fight over Christianity on the island of Mactan. The Chief of Mactan refused to convert to Christianity, so Magellan and about 60 of his men tried to punish the islanders. A mass of villagers—armed with iron-tipped bamboo spears, arrows, and stakes—attacked Magellan and his men.

WONDER WHY?

Magellan lost his life in a battle over religion. Many Renaissance explorers tried to convert others to Christianity or wipe out people of other religions. Do you think such behavior was reasonable or acceptable? Why or why not?

In the violence that followed, Magellan was killed. It was a gruesome death. Some say that the Mactan islanders kept pieces of his body.

What happened after Magellan died? Off the coast of the Philippine island of Bohol, the *Concepción* was burned. Magellan's remaining sailors did not want the ship to be captured.

The last two ships and surviving sailors finally arrived at Tidore in the Moluccas on November 8, 1521. The men loaded the ships with cloves, hoping to make some money and ensure that their mission achieved another of its goals. After loading up, the two ships headed in different directions.

CONNECT

Watch a video about Magellan here. Why is he considered one of the most important explorers in history?

 PBS Magellan video

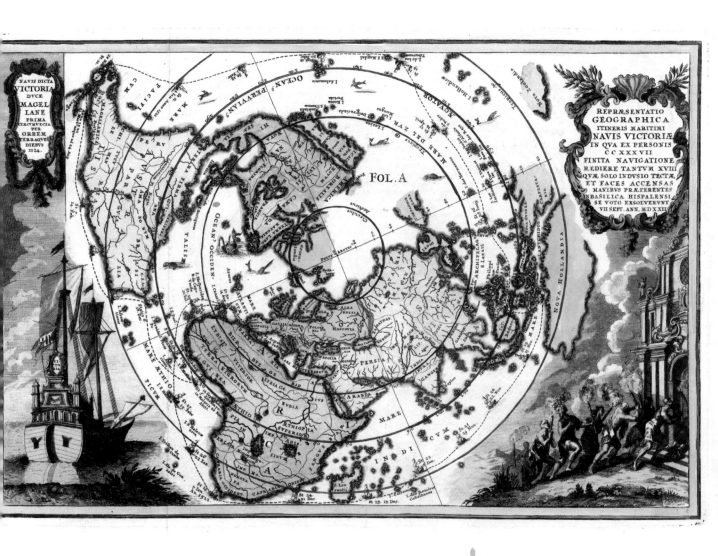

Juan Sebastian Elcano (1476–1526) commanded the *Victoria*. He and his men, including Pigafetta, departed for Spain via the Cape of Good Hope on December 21, 1521. They arrived back in Spain on September 8, 1522—and so completed the first circumnavigation of the world. Only 18 members of the original crew made it all the way around the earth.

A 1700 map of Magellan's journey
By Heinrich Scherer (1628-1704)

The *Trinidad* left the Moluccas, and planned to head back to Spain the way it originally came. The ship, however, was captured by the Portuguese. Eventually, four survivors from the *Trinidad* made it back to Spain via India.

What Makes Him Different?

Ferdinand Magellan was different from many of the Renaissance explorers in several ways. For one thing, Magellan's most famous expedition was not for the country of his birth but for his new homeland.

This was unusual in the Renaissance. Explorers were often very loyal to their home countries. Also, instead of sailing east from Europe to Asia, Magellan decided to sail west. This was a radical idea at the time.

A statue of Magellan in the Monument to the Discoveries in Lisbon

credit: christopher_ brown (CC BY 2.0)

Lasting Legacy

Ferdinand Magellan was one of the most important Renaissance explorers. His expedition was the first to sail all the way around the world. The knowledge gained during this expedition really improved how Europeans understood the planet. It showed how large the earth was. It also introduced several animals unknown to Europeans at the time, such as fur seals and Magellanic penguins.

Thanks to Magellan's groundbreaking voyage, the Strait of Magellan—as it is now known—just off South America's southern coast, became an important route for navigation. Because of his team's efforts, world maps became much more accurate after Ferdinand Magellan's expedition.

WORDS OF WONDER

What vocabulary words did you discover? Can you figure out the meanings of these words by using the context and roots? Look in the glossary for help!

negotiation · convert
malnutrition · circumnavigation
rations · mutiny

Create a Travel Board Game

Many board games feature adventures and travel. What about designing a board game around the theme of Magellan's voyage? Players will see what it's like to be a Renaissance explorer!

> **Look at a variety of board games to get inspiration.** Notice the design of the boards and playing pieces. Glance over the instructions to see how they are played.

> **Be sure to gather some information about Magellan's voyage before starting to create your game.** You'll want to know places he visited, as well as good and bad events that happened on the journey.

> **Design your game board using cardboard or poster paper, markers, paint, small objects, and anything else you might want.** For example, you might want to create a series of squares on the board that players have to move along. A square on the board might read, "You hit a storm, move back 3 spaces" or "You find fresh water, move ahead 2 spaces."

> **On a piece of paper, write down the rules for your game.** It's important all players understand the rules.

> **With family members or friends, try out your new game.** Was it easy to play? Feel free to adjust the game as needed. Have fun!

Try This!

> **What other type of game can you create?** Can you brainstorm a role playing game, a video game, or a card game?

What You Need

2 clean, empty 2-liter soda bottles, water, glue, scissors, duct tape

Create a Hurricane

Many of the Renaissance explorers got caught in nasty storms as they braved the open seas. You can create your own hurricane!

> **Pour about 25 ounces of water into one of the empty soda bottles.** It should be three-quarters full.

> **Flip over the empty soda bottle and place it on top of the water-filled one.** Using glue, attach the two bottles together at their openings. Let the glue set before the next step.

> **Cut a piece of duct tape so that it is large enough to place on top of the two bottle openings (which you already glued together).** This will make the seal watertight.

> **Flip the bottles over.** Quickly rotate the top bottle (the water-filled one) in either a clockwise or counterclockwise direction. This will cause a vortex to form. Sometimes large thunderstorms can come together over the ocean, causing the water to start to swirl like a vortex. If the vortex becomes strong enough, it's known as a hurricane.

Hurricane Katia in 2011

credit: NASA image courtesy MODIS Rapid Response Team, Goddard Space Flight Center

GLOSSARY

Age of Discovery: the time from the mid-fifteenth century to mid-sixteenth century when many expeditions left Europe to explore the world.

ambassador: someone who represents his or her country.

archaeology: the study of ancient people through the objects they left behind.

archipelago: a group of islands.

architecture: the style or look of a building.

astrolabe: a device that measures the altitude of the sun or a star to determine latitude and time.

astronomy: the study of stars, planets, and space.

barter: to trade by exchanging one good or service for another.

bazaar: a market made up of rows of shops or stalls, sometimes specializing in one thing.

bias: a way of looking at or thinking about something that might be wrong or unfair or limiting.

botany: the study of plants.

brutality: great physical and mental cruelty.

bubonic plague: a deadly infectious disease carried by rats and mice that can spread to humans. Also called the Black Death.

Buddhist: a follower of the religion of Buddhism.

butt: a cask, typically used for wine, beer, or water that holds about 126 gallons.

CE: put after a date, CE stands for Common Era and counts up from zero. BCE stands for Before the Common Era and counts down to zero. These are non-religious terms that correspond to AD and BC. This book was printed in 2018 CE.

cannibalism: humans eating other humans.

caravan: a group of travelers and pack animals on a journey.

caravel: a small Portuguese or Spanish sailing ship, usually with triangular sails on two or three masts.

cartographer: a person who makes maps.

chaos: a state of confusion.

chivalry: the customs and ways of knighthood.

Christian: a person who follows the religion of Christianity. Its central belief is that Jesus Christ is the son of God.

circumnavigation: traveling completely around something, such as the earth.

city-state: a city and its surrounding area, which rules itself like a country.

civilization: a community of people that is advanced in art, science, and government.

climate: the weather patterns in an area during a long period of time.

coat of arms: a design made of several symbols that represents a family or country.

colonization: when a group of people settle in a new place, taking control of it and eventually calling it their own.

colony: a group of people who form a settlement in a distant land, but remain under the control of the government of their native country.

compass: a device that uses a magnet to show which direction is north.

compass rose: a circle drawn on a map to show north, south, east, and west.

conflict: disagreements that can be verbal or physical.

conquer: to defeat someone or something.

convert: to change a person's religious beliefs.

corpse: a dead body.

cosmographer: a person who studies the general features of the universe.

cubit: an ancient unit of length equal to about 18 inches.

culture: the beliefs and way of life of a group of people, which can include religion, language, art, clothing, food, holidays, and more.

currency: money or other valuable items used for exchange.

current: the steady flow of water or air in one direction.

customs: traditions or ways of doing things, including dress, food, and holidays.

dhow: a ship with one or two masts and triangular sails, used in the Indian Ocean.

dictator: a person who rules with complete authority, often in a brutal or cruel manner.

diorama: a scenic representation where lifelike figures and surrounding details are set, often against a painted background.

diplomatic: concerned with communication between countries.

diverse: many different people or things.

doldrums: parts of the ocean close to the equator that are known for their lack of winds.

duty: something that one is expected or required to do.

edible: safe to eat.

embassy: a group of people appointed to undertake a diplomatic mission.

empire: a group of countries, states, or lands that are ruled by one ruler.

epidemic: a disease that hits large groups at the same time and spreads quickly.

equator: the imaginary line around the earth halfway between the North and South Poles.

etiquette: accepted code of public behavior.

expedition: a difficult or long trip taken by a group of people for exploration, scientific research, or war.

export: goods sent to another country to sell.

ferment: when a substance breaks down over time into another substance, such as grape juice turning into wine.

flagship: the ship in a fleet that carries the commander.

fluent: able to express oneself easily in another language.

gale: a very strong wind.

Gold Coast: a region of western Africa on the northern shore of the Gulf of Guinea.

goods: things for sale or to use.

GPS: Global Positioning System, a system of satellites, computers, and receivers that can determine the exact location of a receiver anywhere on the planet.

gruesome: something horrible and bloody.

Hindu: a follower of Hinduism, a group of religious beliefs, traditions, and practices from South Asia.

hostage: a person held against their will by another person or group in order to ensure demands are met.

hull: the main body of the ship that includes the bottom, sides, and deck.

humanism: a belief that human beings can improve themselves and their world through a rational approach to problem solving.

hurricane: a bad storm with high winds.

incense: a material that is burned to produce a pleasant smell.

indigenous: describes a person who is a native to a place.

inlet: a small body of water that leads inland from a larger body of water.

intellectual: a person who is engaged in learning and thinking.

investment: a purchase made by a person in hopes of a larger future return.

itinerary: a planned route or journey.

junk: a ship from eastern Asia with a high stern and sails with four corners.

keel: a ridge that runs the length of a boat's hull.

lagoon: a stretch of salt water separated from the sea by a low sandbank or coral reef.

Latin: the language of ancient Rome and its empire.

latitude: an imaginary line around the earth that runs parallel to the equator. It measures your position on the earth according to the equator.

literature: written work such as poems, plays, and novels.

longitude: the distance of a place east or west of the prime meridian, an imaginary line that runs from the North Pole to the South Pole.

malnutrition: poor nutrition caused by not eating the right foods.

maneuverability: the ability to move easily and switch directions.

maritime: related to the sea, sailing, or shipping.

mausoleum: a large, official tomb.

medieval: from the Middle Ages.

memoir: a historical account or biography written from personal experience or knowledge.

merchant: a person who buys and sells goods for a profit.

Middle Ages: the period between the end of the Roman Empire and the beginning of the Renaissance, from about 350 to 1450 CE. It is also called the Medieval Era.

minerals: naturally occurring solids found in rocks and in the ground. Rocks are made of minerals. Gold and diamonds are precious minerals.

mission: the goal of a person or organization or a group sent to perform a service or carry on an activity.

missionary: a member of a religious group who is sent into another area to perform works of service and to spread the word about their religion's teachings.

monarch: a hereditary leader, such as a king, queen, or emperor, who rules a country.

monopoly: complete control of something, such as a service or product.

monsoon: a seasonal wind that reverses direction between summer and winter and often brings heavy rains. Monsoons are most common in Asia, Mexico, and the southwestern United States.

Moors: people from North Africa.

mosque: a Muslim place of worship.

motive: a reason for doing something.

mourn: to show sadness about someone's death.

mouth: the point where a river empties into a larger body of water, such as an ocean or sea.

Muslim: a person who follows the religion of Islam.

mutiny: an open rebellion by soldiers or sailors against their commanding officers.

nautical: relating to ships, shipping, sailors, or navigation on a body of water.

navigation: finding your way using stars, maps, landmarks, and other tools.

Negev: a desert region in southern Israel.

negotiation: a discussion aimed at reaching an agreement.

New World: the land now made up of North and South America. It was called the New World by people from Europe because it was new to them.

noble: in the past, a person considered to be of the most important group in a society.

padrão: a stone marker often placed to claim land by Portuguese explorers.

page: a boy who acted as a knight's apprentice.

palm: a tropical tree with fronds.

patron: a person who gives financial support to a person or organization.

peasant: a farmer during the Middle Ages who lived on and farmed land owned by his lord.

penance: punishment dictated by the Church.

Persian: a native or inhabitant of ancient or modern Persia (or Iran), or a person of Persian descent.

phenomenon: something seen or observed.

pilot: someone who leads a ship through a difficult or dangerous area of water.

philosophy: the study of truth, wisdom, the nature of reality, and knowledge.

pilgrim: a person who travels for religious reasons.

pope: the head of the Roman Catholic Church.

prestigious: something inspiring respect and admiration.

primary source: an original document or physical object created during the event or time period being studied.

prime meridian: the imaginary line running from the North Pole to the South Pole through Greenwich, England. The line divides the world into the Eastern and Western Hemispheres.

provisions: food, drink, or equipment for a long journey.

pyre: a heap of wood used for burning a dead body.

radical: extreme.

rations: someone's share of food.

Renaissance: the period in European history between the 1300s and 1700 that was marked by dramatic social, political, artistic, and scientific change.

renounce: to give up.

resin: a sticky liquid made by trees.

retaliate: to fight back.

ritual: a series of actions or behaviors regularly followed by someone, often as part of a ceremony.

scholar: a person who studies a subject for a long time and knows a lot about it.

scurvy: a disease caused by lack of vitamin C, with symptoms of weakness and bleeding gums.

seafaring: traveling by sea for work or recreation.

siege: surrounding a place, such as a city, to cut off supplies. It forces those inside to eventually surrender.

sonar: a system used to measure the depth of water by using sound waves.

sponsor: to provide funds for a project or activity.

squire: a person who carried the armor or shield of a knight.

strait: a narrow passage of water that connects two larger bodies of water.

strive: to make a great effort.

subcontinent: a large area of land that is smaller than a continent.

sultan: a ruler or king, especially of a Muslim state.

tax: an extra charge added to the price of something.

technology: the tools, methods, and systems used to solve a problem or do work.

teff: an African cereal grown almost exclusively in Ethiopia.

territory: an area of land.

textile: cloth or fabric.

trade: the exchange of goods for other goods or money.

trade route: a route used mostly to carry goods from one place to be sold in another.

trade wind: a wind that blows almost continually toward the equator from the northeast north of the equator and from the southeast south of the equator.

trial-and-error: trying first one thing, then another and another, until something works.

trinket: a small ornament or object of little value.

values: strongly held beliefs about what is valuable, important, or acceptable.

Venetian: describes someone from Venice, Italy.

viceroy: the governor of a province or country who rules as the representative of a king or sovereign.

vortex: a rapidly spinning current of water or column of air.

wealth: money and valuable belongings.

RESOURCES

BOOKS

Adams, Simon, R.G. Grant, and Andrew Humphreys. *Journey: An Illustrated History of Travel*. DK Publishing, 2017.

Burnett, Betty. *Ferdinand Magellan: The First Voyage Around the World*. The Rosen Publishing Group, Inc., 2003.

Elliott, Lynne. *Exploration in the Renaissance*. Crabtree Publishing Co., 2009.

Explorers: Tales of Endurance and Exploration. DK Publishing, 2010.

Landau, Jennifer. *Vasco Da Gama: First European to Reach India by Sea*. Rosen Publishing, 2016.

WEBSITES

Age of Exploration: Austin Community College
sites.austincc.edu/caddis/age-of-exploration

The Age Of Exploration: History Channel
history.com/shows/mankind-the-story-of-all-of-us/infographics/age-of-exploration

Exploration And Trade: Annenberg Learner
learner.org/interactives/renaissance/exploration

Ferdinand Magellan: Kids Past
kidspast.com/world-history/ferdinand-magellan

Renaissance: Kids Discover
online.kidsdiscover.com/unit/renaissance

Renaissance civilization: BBC
bbc.co.uk/schools/gcsebitesize/history/shp/middleages/earlymoderncivilisationrev1.shtml

The Renaissance In Italy: Kids Past website
kidspast.com/world-history/the-renaissance-italy

RESOURCES

QR CODE GLOSSARY

PAGE 4: youtube.com/watch?v=OH7wD_xKOE8

PAGE 23: archive.org/details/NicoloDeContisEarlyFifteenthCenturyTravelsInTheEast

PAGE 39: youtube.com/watch?v=-n7Cb6KF7dI

PAGE 50: youtube.com/watch?v=rxHf_2zTcQo

PAGE 53: wdl.org/en/item/10068

PAGE 55: burtoniana.org/books/1880-Os%20lusiadas/Os%20lusiadas%20Vol%201.pdf

PAGE 56: esmeraldashipwreck.com

PAGE 74: wdl.org/en/item/1058

PAGE 83: youtube.com/watch?v=Y94s85-Crew

PAGE 84: nationalgeographic.org/thisday/jun7/treaty-tordesillas

PAGE 91: youtube.com/watch?v=ScsguX-zqeM

PAGE 92: brbl-dl.library.yale.edu/vufind/Record/3438401

PAGE 94: vermont.pbslearningmedia.org/resource/
pbs-world-explorers-ferdinand-magellan/pbs-world-explorers-ferdinand-magellan/#.WtYGUNPwaL8

INDEX